An Exploration of Spiritual Diversity in America's Heartland

by
John Henry Clark III

Copyright © 2014 John H. Clark III

Publishing services provided by Archangel Ink

ISBN: 1942761600
ISBN-13: 978-1-942761-60-0

This book is dedicated to my family, my friends, and in loving memory of my mother, Billie Jo, who died June 15, 2000, after an agonizing struggle with cancer. She was special, and I miss her all the time. If there indeed is such a place as heaven, she is surely there.

Introduction

Spiritual beliefs across the country are as varied as the vast rugged, rolling, boggy, barren, sandy, stony, wooded, windswept and always beautiful terrain that it contains.

Just as one can find anything from warm Gulf of Mexico beaches to pristine freshwater lakes; wide, flowing rivers and quiet, soothing streams; thick, cool forests, arid deserts and jagged mountains, probably any and all manner of spiritual belief and worship can be found as well, for those willing to look hard enough.

During the summer of 2004 and another week in July 2005, I spent a total of about four weeks crisscrossing Texas, visiting scores of small towns and large cities, asking people what they believe in and why. My intention was to not only find answers for my own questions about the meaning of life, but also to share those answers with other people, in hopes that someone else might benefit from what I learned.

Most all the interviews occurred by virtue of purely random selection. I simply picked a destination, headed that way and stopped whenever and wherever I spotted someone who seemed a likely candidate. It is not an easy thing, walking up to complete strangers and asking them to talk about something so personal as spiritual belief. But beginning with my very first interview outside the San Saba County Courthouse in central Texas, most everyone I ran into was willing to sit with me for a half-hour or more to talk about their beliefs; probably only a dozen or so people ever turned me down. One person even tracked me down after he changed his mind about initially turning down my interview request. Not only did such kindness and cooperation make writing this book possible, it also served to reassure me of the overall goodness of not only this state's 21 million residents, but also the loving nature of mankind in general. Thanks again to all those who participated.

One important thing I quickly discovered after beginning this project was that it would produce much more than simply a collection of stories about spirituality. More than that, it laid bare the souls of a wide variety of human beings from all walks of life -- ministers, businessmen, truck drivers, produce vendors, retired construction workers, artists, craftsmen, journalists, college professors, recovering drug addicts, alcoholics, oilfield workers, spiritual healers – and revealed not only their humanness, but also their commonality. People told me moving stories of tragedy and triumph, disappointment and fulfillment, shattered dreams and restored hope. No matter their social status, socioeconomic level, education, race or gender, all these people share the same basic desires: love and happiness, comfort, safety and security.

All the names in these stories are authentic. However, ages of the participants will obviously have changed since they were interviewed in 2004 and 2005.

This book began as part of an ongoing search for meaning that I have undertaken since becoming somewhat disillusioned with my own religion in recent years. I discuss that journey in detail in the last chapter, warts and all. In doing so, I make public some of the deeper, darker secrets in my life history that previously were known to fewer than a handful of people. That was a scary thing to do. But to do less would be less than honest.

My sincere hope for this work is that others who are also searching for spiritual and other truths will see something of themselves in one or more of the stories here, including mine, and maybe find some answers of their own along the way.

May God bless us, each and every one.

Table of Contents

Chapter 1 – John Short: "I believe there are angels walking the Earth right now... I don't have any doubt in my mind."

Chapter 2 – Barbara Broadright: "When my son died... I blamed God for a long time... "

Chapter 3 – Beryl Battise: "We don't pray to the rain gods, or the wind gods, or any of that... we have one God, and he provides everything."

Chapter 4 – Jim McBrayer: "I sure don't believe in hell. The idea that God would create humans and then put them in hell forever and ever and torture them for all eternity? What a ridiculous concept of God... "

Chapter 5 – Curtis Smith: "Maybe sometimes you've got to get really tired before you wake up."

Chapter 6 – Mohan T. Bhakta: "God does not punish people..."

Chapter 7 – Sister Margie Silguero: "Life is never easy. You will struggle at times, no matter what you're doing. But there are always other people who have situations that are worse... and I believe that, no matter what, God is there to show me the way and uplift me."

Chapter 8 – M Martin Jr.: "Lot of people say life is hard, but life is kind of simple, really. It's just work. Life is work. If you want something, you've got to work for it."

Chapter 9 – Sig Christenson: "I think when you come to the end of your life, the thing that matters maybe more than anything else is that you have been honest. If you spend your whole life bullshitting yourself and everyone else, I don't think God's going to be very happy with you. God expects more out of you than that."

Chapter 10 – Betty Middleton: "I believe if you die and you're saved, you go to heaven; if you're not saved, you're going to go to hell. Plain as that."

Chapter 11 – Jake Lozano: "Sometimes I do think there is a God, but most of the time I don't."

Chapter 12 – Chris Hensley: "It just took a lot of being broken by the world, until I realized, 'OK, this is not all there is, just getting drunk and high. There's got to be something different.'"

Chapter 13 – Tom Davis: "I don't use the word God, because the Christians have a trademark on that, and what they mean by it is not what I mean by it."

Chapter 14 – Allen Archer: "In certain aspects, that little spark that keeps us alive is God... so there's a little bit of him in all of us. Kind of like if you take a drop of water out of the ocean – the ocean is God, and we're like a tiny drop of water out of the ocean."

Chapter 15 – Russell Craft: "It was just so natural at the time, it didn't even hit me that I was hearing God's voice speak to me. I just answered him. It wasn't until afterward that it dawned on me, 'That was really weird.'"

Chapter 16 – Jeri Hyde: "I think you are a spiritual being, having a physical experience right now. And you're going to continue to be a spiritual being...I don't think I'm going to die; I don't think any of us do, because you can't destroy energy. That's what we are, energy."

Chapter 17 – Jesse "Black Bear" Camacho: "When I wake up in the morning, I burn my sage and I give thanks for the sun coming up, the air that fills my lungs, a good night's sleep and pleasant dreams, and for the privilege of walking on the Earth for one more day. I say my prayers to the four directions, asking the spirit of the four directions to guide me today, to be a better person than I was yesterday and the day before."

Chapter 18 – Dan Housley: "... I knew that if anything happened to me, I was going to heaven."

Chapter 19 – Jerome Denmon: "I was walking across the street to my truck, and I told the Lord that my life was his."

Chapter 20 – Roy Bean: "When I was a kid, I was raised in a Pentecostal church... it wasn't an option. I tell everybody I had a 'drug problem' – my grandmother and my mother drug me to church."

Chapter 21 – Julie Palmer: "The significance of life for me is the joy in living it... when I open myself up to everything that I am feeling – the sadness of having lost something, the tremendous embarrassment of having said something – when you get to that depth, that much openness, God is waiting for you inside of that."

Chapter 22 – Shane Johnson: "If God can take a person like me and turn me around, he can do it for anybody."

Chapter 23 – Bobbie Williams: "You can live in hell for eternity, or you can live in the streets of gold, and never have no pain and never be hungry. It's all up to you; it's that simple."

Chapter 24 – Chris Sammons: "The emptiness that I felt on the inside, I wanted to be felt somewhere on the outside. And the only way I knew to try and do that was possibly through suicide."

Chapter 25 – Rev. John Benson: "I think life is a school. We're here to grow and to learn, but mainly to love. Love is the power; God is love."

Chapter 26 – Bill Douglas: "God is the pure essence of love... "

Chapter 27 – John Clark: "I don't know what God is..."

Chapter 1

"I believe there are angels walking the Earth right now... I don't have any doubt in my mind."

Tears slide slowly down his 81-year-old cheeks as John Short recalls the story of an incredible rescue from behind enemy lines during World War II. Trapped deep inside German-occupied territory, he and nine other men were suddenly led to safety by what he says was an angel sent from heaven.

"You can see how much it still affects me," Short said, pausing to wipe a tear from his chin. "I know it is a crazy story, and I've only told it to about three people, but it is absolutely true.

"I'm sure that I've seen an angel on Earth. It still puzzles me somewhat, but I know it made my faith stronger. I have learned that God loves the sinners as much as he loves the saints."

Short, a longtime Lufkin resident who was born near the Texas Gulf Coast in Angleton, served during the war with the 29th Infantry Regiment from Fort Benning, Ga. He crossed enemy lines 36 times on reconnaissance missions, including one assignment when he spent 16 days in hostile territory secretly scouting German troop movements.

"If they'd have over a certain amount of (U.S.) casualties, they'd want to know whether the officers made a mistake, or if the intelligence was wrong," Short explained. "I was pretty good in the woods – I was raised on a farm, and hunted and fished all my life."

It was Christmas Eve night, during the historic Battle of the Bulge in 1944, when the 21-year-old soldier found himself trapped with nine other American troops 60 miles behind German lines in Belgium. The group huddled inside a toll booth as a steady stream of enemy tanks rumbled past on both sides. The tank traffic was so heavy there was no chance for the men to slip out undetected and make their way to safety.

"We knew the route to get out," Short says, "but we had to wait for a break in the traffic.

"Then about midnight that night, there was an officer – a lieutenant -- who just opened the door and walked in... he had on officer pants and clean garrison clothes, a garrison cap. All of a sudden, it seemed like an eerie light was in the room, and he said, 'I was sent here to get you out. And we're going to sing a Christmas carol.'

"Now, normally, if someone had jumped up on a counter – like he did – and started singing, you would have snatched them down and put your hat over their mouth, and wanted to know where they were from and what they were doing. But nobody said a single word. So he got up there and he sang, 'O Holy Night.' Nobody else sang. His voice kind of just numbed us. And when he got through, the traffic outside had stopped. It was gone. And I mean, those tanks had been going through just about like that out there," he said, pointing to a near-constant flow of cars and trucks traveling back and forth along busy U.S. 69, in front of J.R.'s Barber Shop, where the retired mechanic spends a lot of time visiting with the proprietor, Jerry Morehouse, and other friends who stop by for a haircut and conversation.

"Then he told us he would lead us out. We were probably 50, 60 miles from Bastogne, and he said that's where we were going. We went out and we started walking – there was snow everywhere and we were dodging the roads -- and he said, 'I'll break the snow for you.'

"I guess maybe 3 or 4 o'clock the next evening – I didn't have a watch, so I don't know for sure what time it was – we got to Bastogne. It was Christmas Day, and we got in OK; they didn't shoot at us or anything. Then they said, 'Who escorted you in here?' We said, 'He did,' and we looked around, and the lieutenant was gone. Nobody thought much about it. We just figured he must have gone to the officers' quarters.

"Things went pretty fast after that, and around the first of the year or somewhere in there, I got back with my outfit in Liege, Belgium. We were having chow about 9 o'clock one morning, standing in line inside a big, brick wall that ran along a whole block. One of these buzz bombs flew over (a 5,000-pound winged bomb with 2,100 pounds of high explosives), and it hit about eight feet from this Catholic convent, but it didn't explode. One out of every 150, maybe 200 of these things, something like that, would be a delayed explosion, to give time to draw a crowd. Now, the convent was full of 60 of these nuns who were crippled and nearly starved to death. They were in horrible condition.

"We were standing there, and this same lieutenant that I had seen way back on the other side of Bastogne, he walks up and says, 'You have 27 minutes to get these people out of here. Just form a line and hand them out.'

"Now, there were about six or eight of them who didn't want to get out. They wanted to die, and we couldn't do anything about it. So we just formed a line and handed them all out, except the ones that wanted to die. Then, 27 minutes later, the bomb went off. It showered us with brick, but everyone was OK.

"Then after the war, I get out of the Army, come home (to Lufkin) and get married, raise a kid or two – I think I had one child then, and another on the way – and one day they were doing a church survey here. I was a member of the church and I was out doing this survey, and I go into this house – this older couple – and as I was completing the survey, this fellow picked up a Bible and started reading it. And he began to chastise me a little bit. It hit me pretty hard, because I had gone about four years without missing a Sunday school, a prayer meeting, a visitation... I thought I was really something special. To my shame, I thought I was a little bit better than some people. But I was soon to find out that I wasn't.

"About that time, I looked over and there was this picture – and this picture was that lieutenant from the war. The man noticed me looking at it, and he said, 'That's my son. He was killed a week before Christmas in Belgium.'

"I was stunned. I said, "I want my pastor to meet you.' So I left and went back and got him. Now, this was a little green trim house, painted white, yard well-kept, nice and neat. When we got back over there, all we could find was an old house, run down, and those people were not there. I asked the neighbors, and nobody knew who lived there. This was the same day I had been in this nice green house.

"My pastor said, 'You need a rest. You've been working too hard.' And I wondered myself, 'Am I going crazy?' For two days, I tried to find out who lived there. I went to the city and searched the records and everything. I never found out. Then, I decided I wasn't crazy. I knew that I had a spiritual experience, and it was meant to happen."

That whole experience proved a watershed chapter in Short's life, setting the stage for what would become an undying attitude of gratitude, humility and a burning desire to help others. As a child, he grew up in a large family of "hard-shell Baptists," whose monthly gatherings invariably turned into arguments over religion. Because of those sometimes heated discussions, he grew to question the beliefs of fundamentalist Christians, those people who believe "that the name above their door is the only one."

"I have compassion for those people," he says. "I'm sorry for them, but I'm not prone to argue with them. There's many right ways to believe. I don't prejudge anyone.

"I call myself a semi-Baptist, but I really prefer to be called one of God's children. I know there was a purpose for him sparing me. Whether I have fulfilled that purpose, I don't know. I am trying to be an example, to let people see an example (of God's love)."

One way Short tries to spread his message is simply by doing for others. Since his wife of 54 years, Luprell, died several years ago from Alzheimer's disease, he lives alone and maintains a quiet lifestyle in his East Texas hometown of 30,000-plus. Friends, family and church are his primary interests. And when he sees someone in need, he tries to lend a hand.

"I think the purpose of life is for us all to help each other to heaven," he says. "Clothes, money... that don't impress me none. I don't have any money. I give just about all my money away.

"I was standing up here at the service station the other day, and a fella come up and he said, 'I need a couple dollars to buy something to eat.' I said, 'You can't buy nothing to eat with two dollars.' And I just reached into my billfold and gave him five dollars, and I said, 'Now, go on in there and get something to eat. And don't forget to say your blessings.'

"When I see someone who needs help, I help them. I don't ask questions. They're God's children, too. And, besides, he may be an angel -- you never know. I believe there are angels walking the Earth right now. Lots of theologians don't think that way, but I know there are. I don't have any doubt in my mind.

"I think that if we act like Christians, other people will see us as an example, and they will follow that example. Even though we have churches on every corner almost, and they're filled every Sunday, it's Monday, Tuesday, Wednesday, Thursday, Friday and Saturday that people want to see an example. You can see a sermon, as well as hear one. And it's my belief that if they can see an example, they will know there is a heaven.

"God created this world. You can just look all around you and see it. The way things are formed; the seasons of the year. And he has many openings for every one of us, if we'll just say, 'I do.' "

§ § §

Chapter 2

"When my son died... I blamed God for a long time... "

Centerville resident Barbara Broadright was living in Colorado when she received the telephone call with news that no mother wants to hear – her 26-year-old son was dead.

"He committed suicide over a girl," Mrs. Broadright explained. "He put a gun to his head. And I blamed God for a long time for it. I was mad at God for about four years, before I realized it wasn't his fault. He gave my son a free will, and my son chose to do what he done. He chose to commit suicide. We do have that free will. I wish we didn't, but we do.

"Once I realized that he did have a choice of whether to live or die, then I accepted it, and I quit blaming God for it."

Mrs. Broadright, a 58-year-old retired mail carrier who was born in Silsbee and graduated from Smiley High School in Houston, now lives in Centerville with her second husband, George, 66, a retired aircraft mechanic. The couple, former residents of The Woodlands, moved in December 2001 to the town of 903 people halfway between Houston and Dallas along Interstate 45.

Although she grew up the daughter of a Pentecostal preacher and raised her four sons in a Christian home, Mrs. Broadright says her faith was badly shaken by her second-oldest son's tragic death. She recounted the story of that horrible day on a warm June morning, sitting on the front porch of her small church building as her husband steered a riding lawn mower back and forth across the property.

It was back in 1987, and her son, Leonard, was living in Cleveland, Texas, while she and George were living 1,100 miles away near Evergreen, Colorado. It was her youngest son who made that devastating phone call.

"I didn't believe it," Mrs. Broadright said. "Two or three people had to tell me it was true, because I was just like, 'You are lying.' My ex-husband had remarried, and I figured they were just not through hurting me yet, so I just wouldn't believe it. Then, finally, I had to call somebody else, so I called the funeral home where they said he was at, before I even believed it.

"We were volunteer firefighters, and George had gone on a fire call. I had stayed home because I wasn't feeling good or something, and I called the fire department and asked them to radio him and tell him to come home. I was there by myself, and I just had to get outside.

"So I went walking, and I was talking to God. I walked for a good four or five hours, and I was screaming at him, (and) I was cussing him out. I was furious that he let something happen to a child that he gave me. I wanted to know, why not me? You get to thinking about some of the crazy things you've done in your younger life, and you get to wondering whether God is punishing you for the things you did. The Bible even tells us that he could get serious with us and do such, so I thought that for the longest... but in the end, I said, no, God is a loving God, and he would not punish me that way. He does not punish us; we punish ourselves. He is the one that gave me the son, and he would not do this to me. He doesn't make bad things happen, but bad things happen. You just have to go with the flow, and know that he is going to take care of it. Because he's not going to give us more than we can handle. He told us he wouldn't. And before we break, he will pick us back up again.

"I never really backed off from God, but it was just that I wasn't as close to him. I did not walk as close as I should have. I had quit going to church, and quit praying. Then, finally, when I got my stuff together, he was right there waiting for me, as usual. He didn't need me, but I needed him again in my life. I don't know... it just wasn't working anymore, me being mad at him. It was just time for me to get back with the Lord again."

Those were the darkest days of her life, Mrs. Broadright says, and there have been other tough times as well. Her oldest son "has been in and out of trouble since he was 18," and is now serving time in prison. Another son is struggling as well, while her third son has moved past the wildness of his youth to become a responsible husband and father. The way he has turned his life around gives her hope that the others will some day follow suit.

"He is a Christian, and his wife is very religious," Mrs. Broadright said. "I just thank God for her every day. I think sometimes that if it wasn't for her, this one might still be out doing the things of the world.

"It's very hard. All you can do is keep praying for them, and the Lord has promised us that he will answer our prayers. And that's what I have to look forward to – that he is going to. He doesn't tell us when he is going to, but he will answer my prayers," she said.

Her husband is a Bible scholar of sorts, Mrs. Broadright says, spending hours each day studying and contemplating its messages, and she counts on him to interpret and explain the intricacies of the various books and verses. She believes following the Christian faith is the way to true happiness, and following its principles is the way to reach heaven. There may be other truths, she says, but this one works for her.

At one time, her husband practiced Catholicism, and their contrasting beliefs often led to vocal disagreements.

"We used to argue quite a bit about him praying to Mary, and me praying to Jesus," Mrs. Broadright said. "I would ask him, 'Why are you going to Mary? The Bible says you take it to Jesus, and Jesus will take it to his father.' He said, 'Well, Mary will take it to Jesus.'

"And I said, 'No, Mary has nothing to do with it. Mary will not take it to Jesus. And even if she could, why would you want to take the long way around?' " she said, chuckling at the memory. "So finally, him and some guys did start studying the Holy Bible, and now he believes the same way I believe.

"I don't know... I just don't know. Since God is a loving God... I have studied the Bible all my life, but I still really don't know it all that well. I know there are going to be some people turned away, but I just hope and pray that I am one of those who goes to heaven.

"To me, to each their own. But the Bible tells us what God wants and what Jesus wants, and it's just up to us that we read the Bible and discern it the correct way.

"I love him very much... God is my creator; God is my life. There's not a single day that I could go on without him. That kind of sums it up. I'd do just about anything for him. I try to be very obedient to his commands, and obey all his commandments, as much as possible. I know I am a sinner, and I always will be a sinner. But I try real, real hard to do what he wants me to do."

While she has made peace with her son's death, there will always be a hole in her life that can never be filled, and a sadness that never completely goes away. It is her unwavering faith in God, she says, that gives her hope and allows her to live with joy in her heart, one day at a time.

"The Lord has made me strong, and he has blessed us. Without him, sometimes I feel like there would just be no reason to go on. I feel his love; I feel his arms around me. I feel him walking with me. I know he's there, without a doubt. I have to look toward him every time something happens. I can go to him with any problem. I know he may not handle it right away, but I know that one day he is going to handle it for me – in his time, not mine. He is always there, and he always will be there, as long as I am faithful.

"I might get mad at him again, but I won't stay mad as long," she said, laughing. "They say that if you commit suicide, you will not go to heaven. But I have to believe that my son called upon the Lord right before he died, and that he is in heaven. He was a good kid, and he'll always be a part of me. I still talk to him – he don't talk back, but I talk to him – and for my own comfort, I have to believe that he is up there waiting for me."

§ § §

Chapter 3

"We don't pray to the rain gods, or the wind gods, or any of that... we have one God, and he provides everything."

Beryl Battise is a Presbyterian and semi-regular churchgoer, but her strong American Indian roots give her an extended sense of spirituality and worship that cannot be contained inside a building, or limited to religious hymns and Sunday sermons.

"Sometimes I go to church," Ms. Battise says. "I like to listen to singing and to the preacher give his message, but it doesn't have to be confined to four walls -- you can also worship God in tune with nature. You can do it sitting in your yard, raking leaves or whatever. There's the little breeze, the rustling of the leaves, birds singing, maybe some little animals making sounds...that's music, too.

"And if you really look at it, there's all sorts of messages from God in nature: how the wind blows; how it rains; what the birds are singing (and) at what time of day... those types of things can bring messages. So you just sit outside and listen to everything, and it gives you messages.

"Some people say that if you don't go to church, you're not a real Christian. You are living a life of sin. I don't think that is so. It's between me and my God. We understand each other."

That love of nature and its spiritual connection to God stems in part from her heritage as a member of the Alabama Indian tribe, a sub-tribe of the Creek Indians that migrated across the Sabine River into East Texas in the early 1800s, and settled with the Coushata tribe on a reservation about 15 miles east of Livingston.

Born and raised on the 7,000-acre Alabama-Coushata reservation, Ms. Battise maintains close ties with her cultural background by working as a documents clerk in the tribal records department. The 53-year-old divorced mother of four and grandmother is one of a dwindling number of full-blooded Alabama Indians left in the world. As was the case with her ancestors, an active spiritual life is important to Ms. Battise, who refers to God as "Ahbali choo-co-lee," the Alabama tribal name for God, which translates as "the one above."

That is not the actual spelling, since the Alabamas have no written language, but is a phonetic spelling of their word for God.

"He is the one who created everything. He is the one who watches over you, and the one who you give thanks to. We don't pray to the rain gods, or the wind gods, or any of that... we have one God, and he provides everything," Ms. Battise explained.

"Before they went off to war, (Indians) prayed to their god, which was the same as the white man's god. They sang to him, and asked him to look after them. When they came back, they had singing and dancing to give thanks that they were alive. Also, before going out on a hunt, they sang and danced. Then when they came back, they sang and danced again. And it was a religious thing that they did all the time. They had green corn ceremonies, and that was to give thanks for all the things that came out of the Earth and provided for them.

"Maybe some people go to church on Wednesdays and Sundays, and that's the only time they worship God, but to me, when you get up every morning, you're thankful that you're alive. And you say, 'Thank you for looking after me while I was sleeping.' And basically, that's always been a part of the American Indian tribes.

"Whether you are a Baptist, Presbyterian, Catholic, Muslim, Jehovah's Witness, whatever, we are all striving for the same goal, which is to reach heaven and see God. We just have different names for him. Other religions have Allah and Jehovah... just different names."

As a Christian, Ms. Battise follows such traditional religious beliefs as eternal life, and heaven and hell. She is a strong believer in prayer, and having a "personal relationship" with God. Maintaining that relationship is important to receiving answers to one's prayers, she says, since those answers often come unexpectedly.

"I speak to him and he speaks to me. And the message will come to you when you least expect it. Sometimes you will be sleeping and it will come to you. Or you will be at work, or driving down the road. You just kind of pray about things, and later on, you will find answers in a most unexpected way.

"Times in my life when things have bothered me, I have prayed about it, and then when I have forgotten about it, the answer will come to me. To me, it is the answer from 'the one above.' I've never turned away from him. I always knew he would be there to help me over the hurdles that occur in life. I don't think I would have made it through without him."

One of those hurdles came when she went through a painful divorce. It was a miserable time filled with tremendous sadness and loneliness, and she despaired of never finding happiness again. She turned continually to God for help and guidance, and one day her prayers were answered.

"Oh, yes," she said, smiling. "I found a person, my soul mate. He's not Indian, but he's there for me. And he's everything I had always hoped for. Almost close to perfect.

"I went through a very unhappy time, and I know people talked about me, but I prayed. And I always prayed that I would find happiness (again) before I died. Sometimes I would see older couples holding hands, and I said I want to find something like that before I die.

"We have a house together (in Polk County, near the reservation). He's a truck driver and he's on the road most of the time. Some people think we are living in sin, but to me that is where my personal relationship with God comes in. I prayed for happiness, and here he is, my answer. All the bad things that happened to me before, I always said I would forget about it, after I found happiness. And I have – I don't live in the past. I just look forward to the future."

Her liberal spiritual outlook also includes tolerance and respect for most any and all other faiths. Although the Bible apparently tells Christians that there is only one way to reach heaven, Ms. Battise believes there are many paths to the ultimate truth.

"I have my own opinions about what is in the Bible," she says, "And sometimes I don't agree with everything. The Bible was written by men, so how do we really know that all these things happened?

"To me, worshipping your God is a very intimate thing. And if you go around asking people, 'Are you Christian?' – to me that is a very intimate question, almost like asking a husband and wife about their intimate relationship. So the way I worship my creator is basically none of anybody else's business. And I don't go around saying, 'Well, since you don't believe in my God, you're not going to heaven.' That's not so. Each person has their own relationship with God. And he knows whether you're sincere or not. You may go to church and say hallelujah, praise the lord, or whatever, but when you come out and then you put down a person or talk bad about them, you're not sincere. You're just playing with God.

"The definition of a Christian to me is the way you live, the way you act. Like a rich person, for example. He doesn't have to go around showing off his money – you just know he's rich, by the way he lives and everything. So if you're a Christian, you don't have to go around telling the whole world you are a Christian, or take out your Bible and read to them, it's just your way of living that will let people know."

Like most people, her life has seen more than its share of ups and downs, Ms. Battise says. But she is joyful today, comfortable with herself and content in her work. She finds great satisfaction in helping those who come to her small office across the highway from the Alabama-Coushata reservation headquarters. Along with raising her children, she believes she has found a meaningful direction for her life.

"We are here to do something, to help other people," Ms. Battise says. "Right now, I am here helping other people... with their (tribal) enrollment, with legal questions, with papers that need to be notarized, paper work for funerals, things like that. I think I am here to help my people, and to try to lead my kids in the right direction and make sure they are successful.

"I'm not saying I'm perfect – I may do or say things sometimes, and I just have to say, 'God, you'll have to forgive me; I'm just a mere mortal,' " she said, laughing a warm, infectious laugh. "I know sometimes I hurt people's feelings by being kind of outspoken. But I am what I am, and you either accept me or you don't. And I'm not going to change my ways to please you; I'm just me. And I think he knows me and understands me."

§   §   §

Chapter 4

"I sure don't believe in hell. The idea that God would create humans and then put them in hell forever and ever and torture them for all eternity? What a ridiculous concept of God..."

Spending a lifetime reading and studying the Bible, hours upon hours immersing himself in biblical history and research, and untold years faithfully exploring various theologies and religions – including a midlife conversion to Catholicism – led Jim McBrayer to a startling conclusion.

He no longer believes any of it.

"I have decided that God has virtually nothing to do with religion. He's not interested in religion, so why the hell should I be?" McBrayer, a 47-year-old Killeen resident says. "As far as I'm concerned, religion is for the most part about making money off people. They're selling something, and what they are selling is security. I don't care what religion it is, they are saying, 'We have the answers; we have it figured out. We know who God is and we know exactly what he wants. Just put us in charge, and we'll tell you what to do. You give us your money, we'll tell you what to do, and when you die, you get to go to heaven.'

"I sure don't believe in hell," he said. "The idea that God would create humans and then put them in hell forever and ever, and torture them for all eternity? What a ridiculous concept of God.

"That's not justice, for one thing. Let's think of the worst human that ever lived – Adolph Hitler. No doubt he created a lot of suffering, and if anybody deserved to be punished, it would be Hitler. But does Hitler deserve to suffer for all eternity? Eternity is forever and ever and ever and ever and ever. If God is just, if God is fair, you would get what you deserve. No one deserves to suffer for all eternity, not even Hitler. I don't even believe in sin any more. The whole damn thing is stupid. But it's a great way to manipulate people."

McBrayer, a former Army medic who works as a hospital intensive care unit nurse in Killeen, about 60 miles north of Austin, grew up in a strict Southern Baptist family in Marietta, Ga. He and his family went to church "every time the doors were opened," and the precocious youngster developed a regular habit of reading the Bible after he began to detect discrepancies in what some of the adults were telling him.

"I always had doubts about what they were saying. I would get in trouble at church for asking questions, but things just didn't make sense. I noticed that when we did communion, we got a soda cracker and a thing of grape juice – it wasn't real wine. I remember asking in Sunday school, 'Why don't we drink real wine?' And being told, 'Well, the wine that Jesus used wasn't real – it didn't have alcohol in it.'

"I remember thinking, 'That doesn't sound right.' So I knew at a young age that people were going to lie to me, and I was going to have to figure this out on my own. I always read that Bible a lot, all my life."

As he entered his teen years, McBrayer turned away from church and drifted into the drug culture of the 1970s. He retained many of the traditional religious beliefs he learned as a child, but now was discovering a colorful new chemical-induced spirituality, and he also identified strongly with the liberal political views of the times.

"As far as I was concerned, drugs were a mind-expanding spiritual experience that everyone should participate in. And I thought the hippies were the closest thing to God there was. They were against the war; they were for civil rights, women's rights. So I identified strongly with the hippies, which definitely put me in opposition to the Southern Baptist crowd at that time," McBrayer says, laughing.

"I still very much believed in God, and I believed a lot of the Southern Baptist crap – the end is near; Jesus is going to come back. I occasionally went to church. I was worried sick about going to hell when I was a teenager."

By the time he was 20 years old, McBrayer was miserable and at the end of his rope. He was a "deeply troubled" young man, heavily into drugs, estranged from his parents, living with a woman he despised and bickering with his best friend. One day, tired of the whole mess, he quit his job as a security guard, threw a few belongings into a backpack and took off.

With no money, no car and nowhere else to go, he wound up at the local church he sometimes attended. A friend there recommended he go to "this Christian commune-type place," where he lived for a time, until one day he heard a message from God during an emotional, marathon prayer session.

"I was just kind of hanging out at this place, seeing what I was going to do next," McBrayer recalls. "So I was praying and praying and praying, and I remember saying, 'God, I'm not going to leave this room until you tell me exactly what to do.' I was really desperate... desperately needing some kind of assurance that I was going to be OK.

"And I heard a voice that said, 'I am thy salvation.' I actually heard an audible voice. That gave me a feeling of peace about everything, and I got off drugs, got a decent job and started putting my life back together."

McBrayer went on to join the military, later graduated from nursing school, and got married to his wife of 20 years, Jan. A father of one and grandfather of two, he continued his lifelong pursuit of religious knowledge and biblical study, and gravitated to the Episcopal church, where he enjoyed the elaborate, highly ceremonial worship services.

As time went on, however, a combination of increasingly controversial political issues arising in the Episcopal denomination, and his conclusion that Catholicism was truly God-inspired, led McBrayer to become a devoted Catholic convert at age 40. Along with his newfound religious interests, he continued his tireless habit of Bible study and also began to explore other related subjects, including philosophy and physics, in his never-ending quest for self-knowledge.

"Ultimately, it was through reading the Bible and more about how it came about – I went through this period when I read all these books on modern biblical scholarship -- that caused me to question the whole ball of wax. Not just Catholicism, but Christianity – period," he says. "And I concluded that it is a man-made religion that has always had a very political purpose. So eventually I abandoned the whole thing."

One major source of information McBrayer has used in his biblical studies are findings produced by the Jesus Seminar, an international committee of experts including priests, ministers, scholars, historians and linguists that meets each year to consider the authenticity of the Gospels (the books of Matthew, Mark, Luke and John traditionally used to recount the words and deeds of Jesus

Christ) included in the Bible's New Testament. Grasping and accepting their reports was a gradual, at times somewhat reluctant process that rocked his fundamental belief system and changed his life.

"The modern view is, there are very few of the words in the Gospels that scholars think are authentic," McBrayer explained.

"I was totally shocked to find out that Matthew didn't write Matthew; Mark didn't write Mark; Luke didn't write Luke; John didn't write John. Modern scholars believe those books were written anonymously. Nobody knows who wrote them. These Gospels were written decades after Jesus (died), by people who never knew Jesus. They're telling stories that they've heard. And these stories have been colored by different theological points of view. They're not like modern day reporters, who are reporting the facts. They're making a theological point.

"Man, you would not believe how many books I read on this, because I wanted to understand why they say this or that is not authentic – and it made a lot of sense. It really helped me understand where they were coming from. I'm certainly not a biblical scholar, but I've read enough to know that the Bible was written by finite, limited human beings, who had their own agenda, their own program to push. They weren't necessarily telling 'the truth.' They were selling their point of view. And they were not above making things up, if that's what it took to convince other people. The Bible is full of examples of that."

One of those examples, McBrayer says, is the well-known story of the birth of Jesus, which is chronicled in the Bible in the books of Matthew and Luke. Both authors tell wildly different versions of the same event, he explains:

"If we read Matthew, three wise men see a star. They follow the star and it takes them to Jerusalem. The king of Judah at that time was Herod, who hears about these wise men, so he invites them in and asks what they are up to. They tell him, 'We're following a star, and according to our predictions, a king is going to be born.' Herod says, 'OK, follow the star, and when you find him, let me know.'

"So they go on and the star takes them to Bethlehem, where they find Jesus and Joseph and Mary living in a house. Matthew is very specific on this – they are living in a house. Herod gets wind of this and decides that this newborn child is a threat, so he issues an order to kill all the male children two (years old) and under. And you have to ask yourself, why did he choose two and under? That suggests that Jesus may be as old as two years old at this point, so perhaps the wise men have been following this star for as long as two years.

"Well, Joseph has a dream and they run away to Egypt. He has another dream that Herod is dead, and on the way back to Bethlehem, he has another dream that Herod's brother is in charge, so they go to Nazareth, where they live happily ever after.

"Now, the only other story that talks about Jesus' birth is in Luke, which tells a completely different story. According to Luke, Mary is visited by an angel, (and) she becomes impregnated by the holy spirit. Joseph finds out, becomes suspicious, wants to break up with her, but decides to go ahead and marry her anyway. They get married, and live in Nazareth. They end up in Bethlehem because the census goes out from Caesar Augustus. Matthew claims the wise men find them living in a house. Luke has them traveling to Bethlehem while Mary is still pregnant. There is no room at the inn, so they stay in a barn. There are no wise men, no stars, no King Herod killing all the babies. She gives birth, shepherds see a vision of an angel, and they go worship the child. Eight days later, Jesus is circumcised, (and) they go up to the temple in Jerusalem for a purification ceremony on day 40, because that is the Levitical law code. Then they travel back to Nazareth, where they live happily ever after. There's no flight to Egypt, no slaughter of the innocents.

"It is two completely different stories. You cannot fit them together. And this is nothing new. Those first-century Christians could not reconcile the stories. Many theories have been offered, but none of them really satisfy. Almost every single event in Jesus' life, you can sit and compare the Gospels to one another and they contradict.

"If you compare the Jesus in the book of John to the other Gospels, it doesn't sound like the same Jesus at all. In John, Jesus is walking around all the time saying, 'I am the bread of life. I am the light of heaven. I am this; I am that.' In the other three Gospels, Jesus is always saying, 'Shhh, don't tell anybody who I am.' He heals people and then says, 'Don't tell anybody.' Especially in Mark, the earliest Gospel, Jesus does not want a big hullabaloo about himself. In John, all he can talk about is himself.

"In John, the author clearly portrays Jesus as divine. You don't find that in any of the other Gospels. Nowhere, not once, does Jesus call himself God, or the son of God. Go back and read carefully through the Gospels. He referred to himself as the son of man. I think what he meant by that is he considered himself a brother to all, and that's what he wanted people to know. Was he alluding to a passage in Daniel (in the Old Testament)? There's a character in Daniel called the son of man, who appears from heaven and destroys the kingdoms of earth. Was Jesus alluding to that? Possibly, I don't know. But I do know this – nowhere does Jesus call himself God.

"Jesus didn't actually write anything," McBrayer says. "What we have are writings from people who are writing about Jesus. Worse yet, we have people writing about someone they never met. Even worse, they're writing about someone that they've heard about decades later, and you're reading something written by an author who has heard stories told by a church with a definite agenda at stake. And you're reading books that contradict each other, which is a clue... look, these early Christians were not above just making up stories to protect their own interests.

"Each of these Gospels is reflecting the author's point of view. Mark is written around 70 A.D. John is written about 20 years later – and a lot has happened in the church in those 20 years. The Christians have been kicked out of the synagogue; they're not allowed to worship with Jews. There's this big separation between the Christians and Jews. And Jesus has become fully divine by the time John is written. I don't think it started out that way."

While he has firmly rejected the traditional religious views he subscribed to all his life, McBrayer says he is not an atheist, and does in fact believe in God. It is not, however, the popular conception of God as a magnificent supreme being dressed in flowing robes with singing angels surrounding his celestial throne.

"I don't think God is the mythical person of religion. I don't think we should think of God as a human magnified a thousand times. God is not an object out in space. I think God is probably beyond our ability to conceive. We're physical beings, and that is how we try to picture everything. What does it look like? If God is anything, God is inside you.

"Modern physics has shown that basically everything that exists is energy in different form. Energy is neither created nor destroyed. It is just constantly being recycled, and changing form. Our bodies are made of the same thing stars are made of. Everything is made of the same 'stuff.' It's just that at this particular point in time, certain atoms have come together in a particular configuration to manifest as human beings. The stuff that makes up our bodies will a billion years from now be in a totally different form.

"But the important thing is, energy is self-organizing. It behaves in a predictable way. Things seem to be acting according to a plan, which suggests to me that there is an intelligence behind the universe. Behind all this energy, there is some guiding principle. And I think that is God. God is the mind that pervades the universe."

McBrayer, a talented composer and guitarist who has worked as a professional musician and still plays weekends in a local rock and blues band, is nothing if he is not passionate. He alternates between fiery enthusiasm and focused sincerity when talking about his beliefs, punctuating his remarks from time to time with hard raps on the dining room table and the occasional four-letter word to emphasize a point. It was not easy, he says, coming to grips with discoveries that questioned long-held core convictions that gave his life meaning and direction.

"Initially, I was depressed to think, geez, I don't live after death? You mean to tell me that a hundred years after I'm dead, it will be as though I never even existed? My life will have had no purpose at all? Therefore, I said, there has to be a heaven – there has to be. That's what gives our life meaning. But then, I read Nietzsche (the 19th century German philosopher who challenged the foundations of traditional Christianity and morality). Nietzsche got into this, and Christians called him the devil. He was considered the first 'atheist' philosopher.

"Nietzsche tells a story and he says, 'What if a demon were to appear to you, and said that he would give you eternal life. And what that means is, the exact same life you have right now, you would repeat it forever and ever and ever. You get this life forever and ever and ever, or you get nothing. What's it going to be?' Most people would say, 'I'd rather not exist.'

"Nietzsche's point is, to wish anything other than the life you have now is escapism, annihilism. You are looking for another life, something beyond. That's why you turn to religion. You do not appreciate life, he says. You are looking for something else. You're living for this next life. And he felt that's why religion appealed to people.

"His point was, there is no God and this life is all you've got, (so) appreciate it, relish it, experience it, linger in every moment. And if you don't, what's all this nonsense about wanting to live forever? You don't even enjoy the life you're living now, and you want to live forever? That made a lot of sense to me. What are people looking for? They're looking for heaven, where everything's taken care of; there's no problems. You don't have to do anything. Food just magically appears out of nowhere. It doesn't get hot; it doesn't get cold. It's like this desire to retreat to the womb, where you're just oblivious and everything is taken care of.

"I said, 'He's right.' Who knows what happens after we die? I need to figure out how to deal with here and now. There may not be another life. If there is, fine, there's nothing I can do about it. I have no control over it. I need to be realistic and rational, and figure out here and now, and how do I deal with being a human in this life. I stopped worrying about heaven and hell and judgment day and all this other stuff, because if all that exists, it will take care of itself.

"It seems stupid to waste your whole life worrying about the next life. What if there's not a next one? Then you've wasted the one life you had worrying yourself sick over this imaginary life.

"Jan (his wife) thinks I'm an atheist; my parents think I'm going to hell. I keep telling everybody, 'Stop worrying about me – I'm happier this way.' If you think I'm going to hell, I'm sorry you feel that way, but I'll take my chances," McBrayer said, laughing.

"I do believe the universe is unfolding according to some plan, and there is some form of intelligence behind it. You can think of it as a mind, a computer program, an algebraic formula – it doesn't matter. However you want to think about it. There is some form of planned intelligence behind everything. And I believe that the same plan that makes an acorn grow into a tree, the same plan that causes a star to spin off matter that turns into an Earth that gives rise to chemicals that form life, that same process is going on inside you and me. And I think there's a little plan inside each person, and the key is to discover who you are and act upon it.

"Aristotle said the purpose of a human life is to be good. Now, what does that mean? A good hammer is one that nails appropriately. A good flashlight is one that illuminates what you're trying to see. It does what it is supposed to do. A good human does what they're supposed to do. And what they are supposed to do is unique to every person, and it is up to that person to figure it out. I think that's where human fulfillment comes from – being who you are. Learn to be who you really are. Why can't we just be happy with that?

"Dogs are who they are, stars do what they're supposed to do; humans are the only ones who sit around scratching their ass trying to figure out what to do next. Humans are the only animals that ask, 'Why am I here? What is the meaning of life?'

"If I am laying there dying tomorrow, and this is it, I'm glad that I lived. I've known a lot of people. I've experienced a lot. I've been very loved. I've seen beautiful places. I've suffered and I've had pain, but overall my life has been a beautiful, wonderful experience. I learned how to play guitar; I've heard great music. I've read great books. My life was great. I'm grateful for it. And if it goes on, that's even better. If it doesn't, I am glad for every second. It was all a gift to begin with... from the universe, from whatever. If I die tomorrow, never to be heard from again, it was all worth it."

§ § §

Chapter 5

"Maybe sometimes you've got to get really tired before you wake up."

Red, ripe tomatoes; plump, yellow squash; and sweet, juicy melons are not only quality products he offers for sale outside the San Saba County Courthouse, Curtis Smith says the fresh produce items arranged neatly on the tailgate of his truck are an example of God's presence in his life.

"I think the good Lord leads me to buy this good stuff – I really believe he does," Smith, 65, said, one bright summer morning as he and his grandson stood on the downtown square in San Saba, selling fruits and vegetables from the back of his pickup, and talking with customers about an overnight storm that brought a lot of wind but not much rain.

A retired sheet metal cutter from Richland Springs, a town of about 350 people in northwestern San Saba County, about 125 miles northwest of Austin, Smith spends a lot of his time now buying and selling fresh-picked greengrocery – "I don't grow none of it; it's too hard," he said – and chasing after his young grandson. He has two grown children and he and his wife, Delma, a Lampasas native, have been married nearly 40 years. From his perspective, the only way the relationship has lasted so long is with divine guidance.

"The Lord means everything to us," Smith said. "I don't believe anybody can make it, if you don't have Jesus in your life. I ran into a woman up in Cisco recently, and she told me her husband drank himself to death. He was 52. Ain't that awful? She was just broken-hearted, but he just wanted to do things his way.

"I've got the finest wife in the world – she's a smart woman and I still don't know what she sees in me -- and we're doing it our way. We're going with the Lord."

Smith was born and raised with two sisters in tiny Richland Springs, and has lived there all his life. After graduating from high school, he went to work with his father, driving a truck and hauling hay. He was later drafted by the Army and served a two-year hitch in various stateside assignments from 1961-63, including a stint as an infantryman at Fort Hood, the sprawling Army post near Killeen.

Although he attended church all his life, Smith did not become what he considers a religious man until he fell on hard times in his mid-30s, while working at the 3M Company plant in Brownwood, just north of his hometown.

A lifetime of back-breaking labor and a career working 12-hour shifts at the plant where he eventually spent 31 years were taking a toll. Smith says his health was beginning to suffer, and in desperation he decided to turn to God for help.

"I had the best ol' Sunday school teachers when I was a kid, and they worked with me, trying to get me to join the church, but I just wasn't ready," he said.

"Finally, after I went to work at 3M... it got so hard, working 12-hour shifts, it just dragged me down. I got an ulcerated stomach, and I'm going to tell you – there had to be some help somewhere.

Some of them boys out there (at work) were religious, and they'd tell me about the Bible and quote me verses. One day, I just asked the Lord to help me. And, you know, I got all right after I asked the Lord to help me. After that, I decided I'd just join the church.

"Maybe some times you've got to get really tired before you wake up."

Smith says he was 36 years old when he was baptized at First Baptist Church in Richland Springs, where he now is a regular member and attends services each week. He is no Bible-thumper and does not go around quoting Scripture, but he knows how much his life has improved since he decided to put his faith in a higher power.

"I went to church all my life, but I was pretty slow about getting baptized," he says. "I can't tell you what the Bible much says, and I'm not a (church) deacon or nothing, but I like to go listen to the Word. It makes my week twice as easy. After I go listen to that Word, the week just flies by. It's wonderful."

He is a simple man with simple convictions, Smith says. He acknowledges the reality of other beliefs and other religions, but the words written in the Holy Bible contain all the truth he needs. The stories in the Bible seem to make the most sense.

"There's some people that just believes in the sun and stuff. I can't hardly be around people like that," Smith said. "Some of them are good-hearted, but I just can't believe like that. I just don't think there's any possible way it could be like that. I just don't believe it.

"I believe the Lord hanging on that cross is the way we are saved. He died on the cross. He spilled his blood for us, then he come back to life. That's a pretty amazing deal. I think that's pretty amazing – giving up your son like that for us sinners. Would you give up your son to save a bunch of sinners? I don't know if I could do that."

Since he became a Christian, nothing has happened in Smith's life to make him question his beliefs. Not that he has never seen hard times, or seen other people experience life-changing misfortunes and tragic events, but his faith has always remained rock-solid.

"I think (when bad things happen to good people) they're not doing something right," Smith said. "There's this fellow around here... I haven't known him very long, but he seems like the nicest old boy, a football coach. Well, this storm just busted his pecan trees up and, you know, he's not doing something. He's not with the Lord or something. I just don't believe the Lord will strike you like that if you're really religious. I believe he's there to help us.

"But I do think that when stuff like that happens, he's trying to tell us something. I've been around a good while, and if you hit your head on stuff like this," Smith said, rapping his knuckles on part of the wooden, homemade camper shell covering his pickup bed, "then he's trying to tell you something. He's trying to lead you the way he wants you to go."

And that is why you can find Smith parked out in front of the courthouse, always ready with a friendly smile and bushel baskets of tomatoes, potatoes, string beans, squash and melons. He believes it is something he is led to do by a God who loves him, and shows him how to love others as well. And he is convinced that his faith and good works will be rewarded.

"I just feel him in me. Just love, you know," Smith says. "I think it's going to be good to be in heaven. I don't want to be in hell."

§ § §

Chapter 6

"God does not punish people... "

When he retired three years ago from his life's work as a civil engineer, 64-year-old Mohan T. Bhakta could have pursued any number of outside interests – travel, gardening, golf, perhaps?

Instead, he chose to follow his heart and devote his days to becoming closer to God and more involved with his Hindu religion.

Now, Bhakta – a Houstonian who first moved to the United States from India in 1972 – rises early each morning to join other followers in worship services at the Hare Krishna Temple on West 34th Street. A lush oasis of beautiful, manicured gardens in the midst of an aging neighborhood on the city's near northwest side, the temple is a place where the soft-spoken father of three married daughters goes to worship and study and nurture his soul.

"It would be horrible, without my religion," Bhakta said. "For the average person walking on the street who does not believe in any sort of religion, there is no difference between the animal and them."

As a Hindu, Bhakta is a strict vegetarian and believes not only in eternal life, but also in reincarnation, a complex system of evolution and de-evolution in which a person's soul is reborn after death in another bodily form. That new form could be human and it could be animal, or even insect, depending in large part upon the spiritual growth or lack of spiritual growth that occurs between birth and death. What happens to the soul is largely determined by the laws of "karma," which basically follow the principle of Sir Isaac Newton that says every action produces an equal but opposite reaction. In others words, what goes around, comes around. And according to Hinduism, the thoughts and deeds of a person during his or her lifetime determine the ultimate destination of one's soul. Good karma equals a rewarding rebirth. Bad karma could result in degeneration of the soul into a lower life form.

The ultimate goal of a Hindu is achieving "moksha," otherwise known as freedom or salvation from this endless cycle of birth and death, as well as the problems of life that include disease, aging and death. No longer bound by the universal laws of karma, the newly liberated soul is then on its way toward heaven and eventual union with God, also known as Krishna. This union can be achieved through true knowledge (gyana or jnana), devotion (bhakti), or right work (karma).

"There are millions of different cycles of life," explains Bhakta, who says he has lived past lives, but has no recollection of details from those prior incarnations. "Our main purpose as a human being is to go toward God, and if we do not fulfill that, we will stay in this cycle. If you misuse your human life, you must re-enter the cycle.

"Whether you believe in reincarnation or not, that's what it is. In our scripture, it says that at the time of death, whatever you are thinking, or whatever is on your mind, that is what will be your next work.

"God does not punish people -- it is our choice. Whatever we do, that is what we get back. He wants us to obey him; he wants us to love. He is giving love all the time. If we don't want to accept that, and we try to manage by ourselves, this place (Earth) is full of misery. Everybody is going to suffer, because of their past deeds."

Prayer and chanting are an important part of his spiritual life, Bhakta says. Both practices are designed to bring one closer to God, while chanting "cleans and purifies the heart." Also known as a mantra, chanting "Hare Krishna" is a way of directly seeking Krishna, or God. The chant is also referred to as a mantra, and represents a call for divine energy. Becoming more connected with that energy brings inner peace and joy.

Although he is a member of the third-largest religion in the world, Bhakta knows he is part of a vast minority in the United States, where Christianity is the predominant faith. However, unlike many followers of other religions, Bhakta says he does not think Hinduism provides the only road to salvation.

"Belief is not the same as religion," he said. "As long as people follow the original scripture – whatever theirs is – they are doing the right thing.

"There is only one God... different people give him a different name, according to their own beliefs. But everybody is God's servant... everybody has to serve him. That is the main purpose we are here; we have to show love for him, and for all the other living entities. God is within every living entity. He is the one who created every living entity, and we should not kill anything else for our food purposes.

"He is the one who has created the whole world; the universe and everything is created by him. It belongs to him. Nothing belongs to us. He is the sole provider of everything, including us."

That is why Bhakta returns to the temple each day, humbly seeking the keys to happiness through meditation, study and prayer. He knows about other faiths, but has never been interested in anything but the religion of his homeland. For him, Hinduism holds all the answers.

"No, I have never studied another religion," he says, smiling. "I have heard some talks, but never studied. I have never even studied mine completely. Now that I have more time, I am trying."

§ § §

Chapter 7

"Life is never easy. You will struggle at times, no matter what you're doing. But there are always other people who have situations that are worse... and I believe that, no matter what, God is there to show me the way and uplift me."

Sister Margie Silguero has spent 35 years tirelessly serving God and her fellow man in communities throughout Texas, and she believes the condition of one's heart is more important for salvation than the nature of one's religion.

"I think God judges us by who we are, and what we have done with what he has given us," Sister Margie says. "He is a compassionate and loving God. Some of my better friends are non-Catholic; they'll go to heaven. If they live their faith... if they believe it in all honesty and sincerity and truth, why would God not allow them to go to heaven?

"Christ himself welcomed many, many non-believers. He gave them that opportunity to join him. Who am I to say what God is going to do? Who am I to say who is going to go (to heaven) and who is not going to go? God is the only one who does the final judgment.

"I've seen people who never go to church, who probably have never studied their faith, but they are the most charitable people, the most loving people. Why would God not listen to their heart, and see the way of life that they have lived? There's no way God would abandon anybody like that. I will always believe that people who have the goodness of God in their heart... there's no way God can reject them. The idea that God would condemn those people makes no sense whatsoever."

Sister Margie, a 51-year-old bundle of energy who radiates warmth and love, was born near the border of Texas and Mexico in Brownsville, to a family of five boys and six girls. Times were tough in such a large family, but her parents taught their children responsibility, and to love and take care of each other.

"We started working at a very young age," she recalls. "There were 11 of us, and each one of us had to adopt a younger brother or sister and carry them with us through all things. We had to provide for their school supplies, their clothing for school, their birthday gifts, Christmas gifts. We had to help our parents, because it was just too much.

"So I started working when I was, like, 12 years old... at some store like a Dollar General store. Then I went into electronics when I was in high school. When I went into 10th grade, I began to evaluate my life – what am I going to do after graduation? My mother wanted me to be a nurse. So I started doing some checks and balances, and I asked myself, 'At the end of my life, how am I going to look back and see what I have done with it? Is it going to be rewarding or not?'

"Back in kindergarten and first grade, I had two (Catholic) sisters as my teachers. My kindergarten teacher... I looked at her, and she reminded me of an angel. Someone very holy, very loving, very patient. Then as I started growing up, my mother started working at a day care center, where sisters ran the day care. Sisters would come into my house with my mom, and they started inviting me to help them out with transportation and stuff, and I didn't want to. I always told my mom, 'Once they know you can do something, they won't let you go.' Well, this one time they needed somebody to help them out, and they called to see if I would help them, and I did.

"So I decided I wanted to be of service to people. The Lord gave me talent, and I want to share it. So I started looking into different religious orders."

After attending summer school and graduating early from high school, Sister Margie attended a convent in Corpus Christi for four years, then was sent to work in Laredo, where she stayed five years. Then it was on to El Paso for a 13-year stint, followed by an assignment in San Antonio, where she earned a bachelor's degree in religious studies from Our Lady of the Lake University.

In 1996, she was sent to work in Marfa, a town of about 2,400 people in far West Texas that is best known as home of the Mystery Lights, a set of unexplained objects that are visible every clear night in northeastern Presidio County, between the city and Paisano Pass, as one faces the Chinati Mountains.

According to the Handbook of Texas: "At times they appear colored as they twinkle in the distance. They move about, split apart, melt together, disappear, and reappear. Presidio County residents have watched the lights for over a hundred years. The first historical record of them recalls that in 1883 a young cowhand, Robert Reed

Ellison, saw a flickering light while he was driving cattle through Paisano Pass and wondered if it was the campfire of Apache Indians. He was told by other settlers that they often saw the lights, but when they investigated they found no ashes or other evidence of a campsite."

In Marfa, Sister Margie is part of the Diocese of El Paso, which encompasses a rural area of 22,000 square miles. Covering such a large region, she and other sisters are sometimes called upon to lead worship services and ceremonies, when a priest is unavailable. Seeing mass directed by a nun rather than a priest is unsettling for some Catholics, she says, but it is all part of the evolution of the church.

"We don't have a priest here every day -- we don't have a priest here every weekend -- and people will panic. And maybe they'll decide not to come to a service because there is no priest. We say, 'OK, so you do not want to receive the word of God, and you will refuse to receive Christ because a priest is not there. What's more important?'

"You'll have a priest who thinks that the lay person cannot be up on the altar. But the church today invites the lay person to be more active... to distribute ashes, for example. I did that two years ago with the youth. I ask them to help me distribute ashes on Ash Wednesday. And I didn't know how the community was going to take that. I asked those who participated how they felt when they were helping me. They said they felt honored, anointed. That is very powerful coming from youth. And a year later, here comes a letter saying that we should have the lays helping to distribute ashes.

"There are those that will hold onto tradition; there are those who are in the middle; and there are those who will take the jump. But you also have to bring everything together. You have to hold onto some tradition, and you have to be kind of in the middle, but the church is changing in so many ways through the years."

When she considers heaven and hell, Sister Margie says people don't have to wait until they die to experience either one.

"I believe we create our own hell right here, according to how we live our life," she says. "And heaven starts here, also. It's not like you've got to wait forever. You can be living in heaven right now, or you can be living in hell. Our reward will be based on how we live our life.

"The Holy scripture says, 'There is no way to the Father except through me.' That is Jesus speaking. My belief is that the way to heaven is through Christ's teachings, but if we don't embrace Jesus' teachings and his life and the person of Jesus, who people have seen and people have witnessed, how can we attest our love for God, who we can't see? How do you attest that you love Jesus, if you don't love your neighbor? Jesus said, 'I am in he, and he is in me. I am the face of everyone that comes into your life.' People think, 'If I pray the rosary every day, I'm saved.' But then they are unkind to their neighbor, (or) they see somebody in need and they don't attend to them -- what use is that? It's all got to come together some place. If it doesn't come together, then you're a goner.

"Some years back, the church was very structured and there were fine lines drawn. And I think those lines many times divided people. Or made people feel guilty. God says, 'It is your mercy that I want, not your sacrifices. I want your action. Don't give me all these rituals and all these rosaries that your pray, and don't light all these candles for me.'

"We don't pinpoint a location for God. He is everywhere: below us, behind us. God is in our midst right now. People say, 'Am I going to heaven?' Wherever God is, wherever he awaits us, we'll be there. If God is here, we are in his kingdom already. I think it's a matter of who you are as a person, and your attitude. Do you embrace the Gospel; do you embrace your faith? Do you own it? Many people read the Scriptures, but does it become a part of you life?"

Sister Margie's life, meanwhile, is extremely busy. She occasionally takes a day off to unwind and recharge her batteries, but mostly she is hard at work, day in and day out, helping others to try and achieve the peace of mind she enjoys through her closeness with God and life of service to others. It is a labor of love.

"I always tell people, if I had to do it all over again, I would choose the same vocation," she says, explaining that her vows as a nun include a lifetime of poverty, chastity and obedience. "I have no regrets. As a matter of fact, when I think about how long I've been doing this, it doesn't seem like it's been 35 years.

"I know that I am a go-getter, and I love what I do. There have been (difficult) situations, but I think if I tried to look for one that put me under and I had a hard time coming back up, I don't think I could find one. There's been ups and downs. Life is never easy. You will struggle at times, no matter what you're doing. But there are always other people who have situations that are worse. Someone else always has a bigger problem than you. And I believe that, no matter what, God is there to show me the way and uplift me."

For those who struggle with spiritual issues, Sister Margie recommends quiet, thoughtful reflection, and listening to that still voice inside that she says invariably will lead a person in the right direction.

"I always invite people to spend some time in prayer, spend some time in soul-searching. I ask them, 'What is it that your heart longs for?' Look for that; look for the presence of God in their lives.

"God finds us. We think we find God, but it's really God who finds us. Haven't you ever had a day where maybe it is not your best day, and then along comes somebody who gives you that special moment that you needed, and makes your day? God sent that person into your life. Sometimes we think that we are more powerful than God, and God needs us. He doesn't need us; we need him."

§ § §

Chapter 8

"Lot of people say life is hard, but life is kind of simple, really. It's just work. Life is work. If you want something, you've got to work for it."

He has always lived on the same 35-acre tract in Long Lake, a small rural community 11 miles southwest of Palestine in southwestern Anderson County.

M Martin Jr. spent a lifetime working in cotton and corn fields, and operating heavy construction equipment – bulldozers, scrapers, backhoes -- before retiring six years ago. He and his wife, Ollie Mae, raised nine children, some of whom still live on the family homestead along with a number of other relatives, including a brother, a nephew and a lapful of grandchildren. During his 75 years, he has experienced plenty of sorrow, and also lots of joy.

And he has learned a simple truth about life that has endured since childhood.

"Life is kind of whatever you make of it," he says. "You can make it bad or make it good. You're going to reap what you sow. That's what I always had in my mind. That's the reason I always try to do good things."

Martin says he dropped out of school after the sixth-grade to take over the family farming duties full-time when his father went to work for the railroad. He figures he was about 19 years old then, and years of helping out in the fields had left him far behind the other kids in school. His mother died when he was a boy, and he and six brothers and sisters were raised by his grandmother, who instilled in the young boy the strong moral values that would remain with him throughout his life.

"She always brought us to church, and taught us how to live; how to treat people," he said. "We knew how to respect people, (and) I think that's something we don't get today. We've lost that in our society, and it shows."

As he got older and took on more responsibilities, Martin got away from regular church attendance. After he got married and his children started to arrive, he often worked seven days a week, but eventually decided to follow his wife's example and join the rest of the family on Sundays.

"That's probably one reason I decided to start coming to church, so I could be with the children," said Martin, who was baptized sometime around age 25 or 26.

"I just wanted to make a change," he says. "I stopped drinking – I never drank a lot, never went home drunk or nothing like that. I wasn't that type person, to go home raising Cain and cussing. So it wasn't too much for me to change. If you're trying to do the right thing anyway, then it's not too big a change when you start going to church. If you want to do right, you can."

His quiet, hard-working country life was detonated by tragedy the day one of his teenage sons, David, died after being accidentally shot by a cousin. The boys, who were best friends, were playing with a gun after school.

"That's about the toughest thing I ever had to deal with," Martin said, taking a break from a scraping and painting project at his church. "They was always buddy-buddy.

"I was on the job, and they come and got me. I didn't want to believe it. He was all right when I left home that morning. But I knew I had to go ahead on and live, you know... try to do for the rest of my kids.

"I still thinks about it, but things could have been worse. Sometimes, I would say, 'Why me?' Then I got to thinking (that) God always does things for a reason. I just come to accept it, and go on with life. You just have to accept things as it is, and look forward. You can't let things like that stop you from reaching the goal you set. You've got to reach that goal."

That goal for him, Martin says, has always centered around family: earning an honest living, raising healthy, happy kids, and trying to do a good deed or two along the way, enjoying the simple things. Chasing those dreams provided a simple answer to the question, 'What is the meaning of life?'

"God came down here and he set a goal for us, which showed us how to live. Then he left it in our hands," Martin says. "I think he put us down here to take care of this ol' Earth, and do the best we can to make it a better place, and to help each other. I want to be a help to the world, instead of a (hindrance) to the world.

"One thing I am proud of is my kids. They're good kids, successful. Never been in any real trouble. And I give a lot of credit for that to my wife. She was home with them all the time. She didn't work for a public job, but she probably had a bigger job with those nine kids than I ever did," he said, smiling.

"Lot of people say life is hard, but life is kind of simple, really. It's just work. Life is work. If you want something, you've got to work for it."

Although he has been a Christian for about 50 years, and considers himself strong in his faith, Martin says he does not believe he necessarily has all the answers. He says man's search for meaning is an individual journey that can lead down many different paths toward finding the truth. And he firmly rejects the idea that there is only one way to get to heaven.

"I don't believe that," Martin said. "It's according to who God is to you. And who he is to you, might not be who he is to somebody else. So I can't say you've got to do what I do, for you to be saved. I leave that up to God, to make that decision.

"I hear a lot of people say so-and-so and so-and-so is wrong, but I don't believe in that. I believe God is in charge. I can't make no decision for you, and you can't make no decision for me.

"And I think God is whoever you think he is in your life. A lot of people say God is a good God, and Satan is out there somewhere. I think Satan lives within each one of us all the time, just like God does. And the one who gets the bigger control, that's the one that going to rule your life. It's just like... I think about those folks who flew them planes into them buildings up there (in New York City). People say, 'How could God let that happen?' But, you know, me and you can do anything we want to. God left it up to us. If you want to get out here and hurt somebody, you can do that. That's the reason stuff like that happens like it does.

"If you want to do right, you say, 'I don't think God would like it, if I do this or that.' You want to try to live a life that pleases God. But lots of people just try to please themselves, and that's where we go wrong."

He has been married to Ollie Mae for 53 years now, Martin said, chuckling as he explains the reasons the relationship has lasted so long. "I was a pretty good boy. I wasn't no wild buck running around. I tried to do the right things."

As for the story of his life, Martin says he thinks it has been pretty successful so far. Like the famous baseball pitcher, Satchell Paige, who once said, 'Don't look back. Something might be gaining on you,' Martin says he neither looks ahead to the end of his life, nor back at the years past. He has no worries about the future, and no major regrets about days gone by. Keep things simple and live one day at a time is a philosophy he says works well for him.

"For the education I had, I think I've done OK," he says. "If I'd have had a better education, I think I could have gotten further...

"I don't think about (the future) too much. I know one of these days (that) I'm going to die, but I don't worry about it. I figure wherever I'm going, I'm going. I can't say where I'm going, because God is in control of that.

"A lot of people say there is going to be a judgment day. The way I feel about it is... you are

judged every day you live. We are really judging ourselves, because they say God's got that little book (of life), and the way we live is going to be in that book. That's what is going to judge us. I think me worrying about whether something is going to happen down the road, then you can't do what you got to do. Because your mind is not focused on today – it's focused on tomorrow, or yesterday. So I try to keep my mind off of that. And after you're gone, there ain't much you can do about it anyway. The only thing we can do something about is right now, today.

"I once heard an Indian say, 'Don't let the past cloud your future.' I thought about that, and I said, 'That's true.' "

§ § §

Chapter 9

"I think when you come to the end of your life, the thing that matters maybe more than anything else is that you have been honest. If you spend your whole life bullshitting yourself and everyone else, I don't think God's going to be very happy with you. God expects more out of you than that."

He did not experience the horrors of war seen in Vietnam, Korea or World War II, but what he did see as a journalist traveling with the U.S. Army's 3rd Infantry Division during the 2003 invasion of Iraq had a profound and lasting impact on San Antonio resident Sig Christenson's sense of spirituality and purpose.

"It didn't change my (spiritual) outlook, as much as it confirmed the things that I have often already thought -- the things that I grew up on, and the things that I have come to believe," Christenson says. "But it certainly has given me more focus.

"It is an event that I will never forget. It is one of the most profound events I have ever had. I can put the real profound events of my life in this coffee cup, and that one – perhaps more than any other -- has reinforced my faith, and helped shape my determination to do things the right way. I would bet that if you took anybody who was in that war, the vast majority would find themselves to be far more spiritual than they were before -- or to think about it at least more than they did. We all took the same risks... we saw people die, and we lost friends. You don't come back from something like that the same."

A 49-year-old Houston native, Christenson covered the controversial war for the San Antonio Express-News, where he has worked as a military writer since 1997. Traveling with combat forces during the height of the invasion was the fulfillment of a lifelong dream to follow in the footsteps of his hero, Ernie Pyle, the Indiana native who won a Pulitzer Prize in 1944 for his battlefield stories about soldiers fighting in World War II.

The most dramatic point in the invasion for Christenson came on April 2, when the 3rd Infantry Division's 1st Brigade came under heavy fire while crossing the Navit Al Ajil bridge, just south of Baghdad.

That was one day after the brigade blasted through Karbala Gap, a critical point on the road to the capital city.

As an "embedded" reporter, Christenson was traveling in an unarmored, "soft-skin" Humvee with Senior Airman Dan Housley and Capt. Shad Magann, members of the Air Force's 15th Air Support Operations Squadron providing "close air support" for the Army units. Their job was basically to spot enemy positions and call in air strikes ahead of the combat troops.

As they considered the heavily fortified, 900-foot-long bridge over the Euphrates River, Capt. Magann decided he and Housley should be the first vehicle across the dangerous span during what was known as Operation Peach. Christenson, riding in the back seat, had other ideas.

"There were artillery rounds coming in, and we had artillery rounds going out; there were mortars coming in and mortars going out. And we were waiting to cross that bridge, when Shad said we were going to be one of the first to cross. I said (to myself), this doesn't sound good," Christenson recalls, sitting at the breakfast table in his northwest San Antonio home.

"Dan and I were in the truck and Shad took off somewhere. Shad was the captain, and he was in charge, so I went to Dan and I said, 'This is suicide. We're not going to make it to the other side.' I said, 'What do you think? Can you talk to him?' Now, mind you, Dan is a senior airman. He was not an officer. And I had already seen the way Army enlisted guys and Army officers interacted with each other. The Army enlisted guy wouldn't even dream of confronting his boss. If he was told to go, he would just go. That's their training. And I guess that's what you have to have in the Army, but I'm not in the Army. I didn't have to be in there with them, and I was sitting there thinking about it. And Dan starts talking to Shad, who had been an enlisted guy and was a good officer. He would explain why we were doing things. And Shad said, 'Look, we have to get over to the other side of the bridge. We expect a counter-attack and we have to be there to call in close air support as soon as we can. That's why we're going.' And he told me, 'Sig, if you want to go to a better-protected vehicle, I'll understand. You don't have to do this.'

"I sat there, and a little voice in my head said, 'That's a good idea. You should go.' And I just thought, 'No, you've come here this far with these guys, and you settled on that a long time ago. You're with these guys, and you can't leave now.' Even though I thought I might get killed here, I couldn't leave them, because by that time, I felt a loyalty to them, and a bonding had taken place.

"So I said, 'No, I'm staying.' That was the moment I became somebody in Shad's eyes. He was impressed. And even as I said that, that little voice inside of my head said, 'You are fucking out of your mind. You're going to die this afternoon.'

"I thought, 'The sun is going down, (and) this is the last time you're going to see the sun. You're never going to see home again. You're never going to see your dog; never going to see your cat; never going to see your wife," he said, pausing as tears welled in his eyes and emotion choked his voice. "It was damn difficult to go to that place. I'm glad I did, but I don't know if I'd want to do it again. That was the moment where I had to say, 'Where are you in your life?'

"Dan and I said a prayer before we went across the bridge -- he has a bad memory like I do, and he can't remember a damn thing about what he said in that prayer – and then we went across. That's when I just said, 'Well, I'm putting it in your hands now. My life has always been in your hands, and whatever comes of this, that's how I'm settling it, because I can't control any of it any more.'

"I saw this one fighter on the ground – I think he was a Syrian – and he was dead. He still had his AK-47 in his hands, and there was a black scorpion next to him. And the scorpion was trying to run away from the battle. There were dead people all over the place, and I thought, 'Boy, this is as fucked up as any place gets.' I have the tape from that battle, and it was a scary, scary battle. There were a lot of dead people around us; there was a lot of flaming wreckage. There were mortars coming in all over the place, (and) you couldn't tell whether they were yours, or whether they were theirs. There was shooting all over the place. We knew that they had rigged the bridge to blow up – because they tried to blow up every bridge -- and it was like a 400-foot fall if the span went out from under you.

"It took us 10 minutes to cross that bridge, and then we went along a 10-foot high wall for three miles. It was a concrete wall that surrounded a rocket motor plant, where they built rocket motors for their missiles. And we made it. I was amazed. I was ready to pinch myself through my body armor when we got to the other side. And that was kind of the right moment for me to... it was the moment when I had to settle up a lot of things, because I had thought I was not going to be alive in 15 minutes.

"There's a reason all of us went through that battle. When the day comes that we die, that's the day we were supposed to die. Until then, I'm going to use that event to remind myself of what is important. I think when you come to the end of your life, the thing that matters maybe more than anything else is that you have been honest. If you spend your whole life bullshitting yourself and everyone else, I don't think God's going to be very happy with you. God expects more out of you than that."

That demand for honesty has become not only a lamppost for Christenson's life, but also the foundation for a spiritual journey that he says will probably continue as long as he lives. He grew up going to an Episcopal church, attending services every Sunday, going to Bible study class and even serving for awhile as an acolyte, or altar boy.

He believed – and still does – in the Bible, but found his attentions turning elsewhere as he entered his teenage years. Like most young men with raging hormones, he began to take notice of and appreciate members of the opposite sex, and his interest in spiritual issues took a backseat to more carnal pursuits.

"The Bible was a very magical book when I first read it, but the world was a very magical place when I was growing up," Christenson says. "And, of course, later I think I pretty much got so focused on my own selfishness that I didn't think much about any of that. And you should do that when you're young. I was a pretty frivolous kid. I went to school, but I wasn't very serious about much of anything. I didn't want to grow up. I didn't want to get too serious too quick."

After graduating from Lamar High School in 1976, Christenson went on to earn a bachelor's degree in journalism from the University of Houston. He then worked as a reporter for the Tulsa Tribune, Corpus Christi Caller-Times and Florida Times Union, as well as city editor for the Temple Daily Telegram and an associate producer for Channel 2 News in Houston.

During those years, he experienced his share of ups and downs, tragedies and triumphs, wins and losses. Although his religious faith had been pushed into the background years before, those childhood lessons remained with him and he continued such things as nightly prayers, and occasional reflections about spirituality and the meaning of life.

"I've never been a great churchgoer, since I was a teenager," he explained. "But as I got older, I have become much more thoughtful about God, and especially since the war, I've had to think about it a lot. I went from being kind of like a space cadet before the war – being real excited about it – to after the war, having lived this experience where you are forced to confront your mortality every single day, sometimes by the hour and the minute, and that causes you to think, reflect.

"I try very hard to think about things; I try to study them when I can. Debate them. I don't think it is a weakness to doubt; I think it is a weakness to be too sure of yourself. All of life is a constant project of re-education. It should be. Maybe with a lot of people, it isn't -- they get to a comfortable niche and they stay there. I won't be critical of that, but I don't think that's smart. I think you'd better be uncomfortable, to a point. Comfort is dangerous. Once you get too comfortable, then you get lazy. You don't question, and you become an easy mark for someone who wants to manipulate you. I prefer to want to know more. And there will be Christians who say, 'Well, you're not a Christian.' I don't know if I am, in the sense that I'm the kind of Christian that they think I should be.

"I don't know if I'm going to be the corner Baptist church's kind of Christian. And I don't care. Somebody wants to judge me... I can't stop it. But I would tell them that they're not very smart people. They haven't used their heads, and they haven't thought about it.

"I feel very strongly that my spirituality is an intensely personal thing. And everybody is on their own path. You've got to find your spirituality on your own. You've got to believe in God – and frankly I don't think it matters what the reasons are for how you come to your faith. Faith is what matters. That's what is important: you've come to believe there is a God, and hopefully you have arrived at that for the right reasons. Then, you've used that base to kind of guide how you live your life."

As for his core beliefs, Christenson holds on to those Christian teachings of his youth. He does not, however, consider himself a traditional, or mainstream Christian. His views might not be well-received in the typical Christian church, but says he doesn't worry about that. Instead, it is more important for him to think for himself, to study, learn and consider a wide variety of spiritual beliefs, rather than follow a particular organized religion.

"Spirituality is an individual journey, and I don't think people should get hung up on what is right and what is wrong," he explained. "I'm not going to make judgments about somebody else's religion, any more than I'm going to make a judgment about whether a Baptist is more likely to go to heaven than somebody in the Church of Christ, or a Mormon. Every religion is created by flawed human beings.

"I know a lot of Christians who look at Mormons and think they're just full of it. And part of it is because it is such a young religion. Well, I'll bet you that's how the Jews looked at the Christians, too, at one time. I think it's a whole lot better to just get away from that. I don't know whether God is going to just take in all the Christians and condemn everybody else... that is what some people believe the Bible says. And Christ says you have to believe in the son of man to go to heaven. Well, I'll let him say that. It isn't my place to say that. I'm not arrogant enough to make that judgment.

"Now, if the pastor down at the corner church wants to say that – in his huge church, with all the money he's making from his business – well, I could judge him, too. Because I don't think the corner church is what Christianity is all about. I don't think Christ made any money out of his ministry. Organized religion to me is troubling. I'll draw the line there and say I'm troubled by it. I'm not going to condemn them for doing it. It's up to God to judge that. And that's why I don't get into this business of, 'you're going to hell.' I don't think people are qualified to do that.

"My experience guides my faith... and my desire to learn and be better informed, and to be rooted in reality and fact, as opposed to wishful thinking. That's important to me, and I don't think it damages my faith. A lot of people might argue that it does damage my faith, but my spiritual journey is unique to me and it is beyond criticism. If you're going to simply say, 'You're doing it wrong,' you'd better do better than that. That's not going to wash. Tell me what I should be doing, and I'll listen. I'll think about it. I'm wise enough to do that. I don't know everything, but it is a very personal journey, and it's not something that is simply guided by one preacher or one church or one set of statements in the Bible. If that means that people look at me as not being a Christian, that's OK. I'm not a

Scientologist, either. It's my journey, and I'm trying to be honest about my journey. That's all I'm going to try to do.

"When I read the New Testament, what I generally like about Christ is that he's almost a revolutionary, in this particular rotten point in history, where people's lives are worth nothing and their lives are not easy. He says, 'If you have two coats and you're brother doesn't have any, give one to your brother.' Well, that's new. There are a lot of supposedly religious people in this country who don't want to lift a finger for people who don't have anything. And I don't know why that is.

"I think part of spirituality is putting into play, in your own life, what you've been taught; and what he is trying to teach you is that you need to care for people. I don't just say I'm going to care for people because he told me to – there are good reasons for it. One of which is I could be one of those poor people. We're all probably just a few paychecks away from being out on our ass. Then what?

"To me, part of what spirituality is, is wanting to make it into the good place (heaven). But to get there, you have to really live it. And the real Christians that I've seen in my life are few and far between – those people who actually put their religion into their daily lives, and even into the words that they say, the thoughts they have for other people. You're not going to make it if you're trying to sell your soul the way some guy has been trying to sell me a car this week. It always starts with integrity. Integrity is above all else the thing that should guide everything you do."

While some may not consider his ideas to be the philosophy of a true Christian, one thing Christenson says he knows for sure is that there is most definitely a God, a creator of the universe and creator of life. He believes in the scriptures of the Holy Bible, but also finds truth in the teachings of Buddhism.

Whatever one's beliefs, Christenson said, he thinks having a spiritual life is an important part of living as a complete and satisfied human being.

"Your spirituality is as much a part of you as your desire to eat or have sex or to sleep," he says. "And it should be. It's part of being a whole person. If you go through your whole life not being serious about your spirituality, you're certainly kind of omitting an entire part of your existence that you should be in touch with.

"I think that is one reason why you see existentialists praising existentialism – because they want to believe. They know at some level why it is important to have some sense of spirituality. So I've come to that point, and I've read the Bible more, because I need to do that. But I'm probably going to read passages from the Buddha as well. I'm going to try to educate myself, because I think that's part of the process. As I said, I try very hard to read and think about things. But it's also real important for me to be honest with myself, and for me to be as honest with myself as I can be is to create a sense of understanding about things.

"I have no doubt that there is a God. I don't have to have a big debate about that. There's no doubt in my mind that all of the universe is the creation of something far more intelligent and powerful than we are. For it to be an accident would be remarkable.

"I believe the universe is so complicated and interconnected that there is no way on Earth that it is an accident. And there's an intelligence to it. So what created it? I don't know how you describe God. What does God look like? I don't know. I think he can look like anything he wants to look like. And if he's in a mood to really scare the hell out of you, he can take that form, too. But I don't know. I'm not capable of understanding the mind of God, any more than Sydney – that really nice Siamese cat over there – can understand my mind. Or any way that a 5-year-old child can understand the mind of an adult. It's impossible. So when Christ says that you have to be like a child to enter the kingdom of heaven, I think what it gets down to is you've got to simply be willing to be that sure on faith, that there is a God and there is a Christ. And that they're both basically one. And that they're in charge, and there is a reason for your existence.

"I think people in every faith are trying to make sense of the world, and they're trying to make sense of their birth, their existence and their death. They're trying to put all of that in one box that explains it for them, and that they can then live in hopes of continuing their existence. I think there is life after death, but I don't know anything. Look, you will never be 100 percent certain – it's impossible. So I'll work under the assumption of being pleasantly surprised. And I don't think it's necessary to have a life after death to believe there is a God.

"I will always be searching. I always want to know more, or understand more," Christenson says. "None of life is getting to this point and saying, 'OK, now I'm done.'

"I think the important thing is that I accept the existence of God, and I am thankful for it, and my guess is that if there are other beings on other planets like us, he is their God, too. Who knows? I have no earthly idea what God is up to, or why we are here. But there is some reason for it. There's just way too much that no one can explain for this to be just some giant accident. So I have no doubt believing there is a God, and if he wants there to be a heaven, there will be one."

§ § §

Chapter 10

"I believe if you die and you're saved, you go to heaven; if you're not saved, you're going to go to hell. Plain as that."

Betty Middleton was always too busy scraping out a living to worry about spiritual issues or ponder the meaning of life, but when doctors told her she had cervical cancer and might not survive, she began to reassess her priorities.

"When you get sick and start thinking you might die or something, then you start thinking, 'Where am I going to spend eternity?' " Mrs. Middleton explained, as she sat shelling a basketful of fresh-picked purple peas in her hometown of Fairfield, a city of 3,200-plus in Freestone County, south of Dallas between Corsicana and Buffalo.

"They wouldn't operate. They said it was too far along for them to operate on it," she explained.

"They just done the (radiation) treatment, is all they done. But I wasn't scared. I just put my faith and trust in God. I never went to church as a kid or anything like that, but I just said, 'God, heal me.' "

It was during that time, as she traveled back and forth to Houston for four months of treatments at M.D. Anderson Cancer Center, that Mrs. Middleton says she began to draw closer to God than ever before.

"You get off down there in Houston, you know, just you and the Lord, and you begin to think and pray... you do more reading of the Bible than you would if you was at home," she said. "I believe God healed me, when I didn't think there was any hope for me. I know he did. It's been since 1985 that I had cancer, and there's been no sign of it since."

After experiencing what she considers a miracle in her life, the 68-year-old Hunt County native became a regular member at Grace Tabernacle Church, a non-denominational Christian congregation in nearby Dew, nine miles south of Fairfield.

Although she did not attend church services regularly as a child, becoming a Christian and joining a church for the first time has changed her life.

"My life has improved a lot," she says. "It made a big difference. I don't act the way I used to – I can't explain exactly what way, just different. I have a church family... it makes a lot of difference, having a church to go to. You get sick, you know, or something like that, they're right there with you, praying with you, different things like that. It's just wonderful. I don't think I could survive without going to church. I don't know how I survived before."

It was that solid faith that helped carry her through another health crisis seven years later, in 1992, when she suffered a major heart attack. At the time, Mrs. Middleton was washing dishes and cleaning tables at a local restaurant, the same job she held during her cancer scare. This time, though, doctors declared her disabled and did not allow her to return to work.

That was a tough blow for a proud, self-sufficient woman who had worked hard all her life, after dropping out of school following the fifth-grade.

"My parents kept me out of school when I was a child, made me work (on the family farm)," she explained. "Then, I also got sick a lot, and I failed so many times – I wasn't no bigger than the other kids, but I was older than all the other kids -- I just quit. Which I later regretted."

One of the most profound disappointments of her life, however, was her inability to bear children. She always wanted kids, Mrs. Middleton says, but for reasons she does not like to talk about, that never happened.

"It didn't hurt me so bad when I was young, but it does now," she says, quietly. "I didn't think too much about it when I was young, but as I started getting older, I started to wonder, 'Why?' You have more time to think about things when you get older, I guess. But, no, I don't question God about that. It's his purpose that I don't have children. There's a reason for it. If he had intended for me to have children, I would have had them.

"I used to think sometimes, 'Why am I going through all this?' All the things I've been through. But now, I realized that God intended it, or he wouldn't have put me here."

Both she and her husband, Gene, 65, of Corsicana, have endured a lifetime of hardship. Gene, who was married twice before, also dropped out of school after the fifth-grade, and went on to work in a variety of occupations, including jobs in a steel plant, fertilizer plant, cotton mill, saw mill and highway maintenance crew. Now that they are both retired, the couple tries to eke out a living growing vegetables at home and selling as much of their crop as they can.

Mrs. Middleton acknowledges that hers has been a difficult life, then grows quiet and quickly resumes shelling peas as the memories come flooding back. Instead of dwelling on the past, though, she tries stubbornly to look ahead and take comfort in her belief that God has a plan for her life.

"I don't like to think back on my life. It's in the past. There's no use in bringing it back up, or worrying about it," she says.

"I don't really think about those things. God knew before we ever were born that we were going to be born. When he died on the cross, he knew we were going to be born here. Sometimes we may not really like that idea, you know – "What am I here for? Why am I having to go through this, that and the other in life?' But I just say, 'Lord, you understand, and you don't put no more on us than we can bear.'

"I just thank the Lord when I wake up, then I thank him at night for keeping his hand on me all day. If we believe in him, he listens. And he answers our prayers, if we're sincere.

"I believe he can save, and he can heal. He's healed me several different times, on different things. I believe if you die and you're saved, you go to heaven; if you're not saved, you're going to go to hell. Plain as that.

"And I need to go to heaven – I sure don't need to go to hell."

§ § §

Chapter 11

"Sometimes I do think there is a God, but most of the time I don't."

Pondering the meaning of life is not the way Jake Lozano cares to spend his free time. The 22-year-old Midland native says he is not the least bit concerned about such things as heaven and hell, life after death or spiritual salvation. For him, the answers are simple.

"I just wake up each day and do my thing: go to work, enjoy my family, go to bed, that's it. That's all I see... life is getting up each day, working, and that's it. That's what you do. There's nothing else in life," Lozano says.

"Sometimes you think, 'How did everything get here?' But I really don't worry about it too much. I really don't think there is a God, or anything like that. It just seems like a made-up story. Buddha has his own story; Allah has his own story. They all have their own story. I just think it's something that somebody made up.

"I've come across a lot of people who have different stuff they believe in, like life after death... and it's real interesting, but everybody has their own opinion on everything. Just like religion – everybody has their own opinion on that. So, it's nice to hear stories from people about what they think happens, and to watch stuff on TV about what they predict happens after you die. That's cool to know, but when you come down to it, nobody really knows. You can't really tell.

"Death is unstoppable. It's going to happen, either way. So I look at it like I might as well just live, and whatever happens, happens. If I die, then I'm gone, you know? It doesn't bother me. I know there's a lot of people who think about it all the time -- "What's going to happen when I die?' I guess I can't just sit there and think about it. Just sitting there and thinking, 'I wonder what's going to happen when I die?' I don't think like that at all."

His outlook, Lozano says, stems mostly from a Christian upbringing in which he says he saw tremendous hypocrisy, dishonesty and worse as a young boy going to church with his family. By the time he was a teenager, he had seen enough.

"The church I went to was, man, just screwed up. Everything was just not Christian-like. They would preach to you, and then go against everything they said. Hypocrites. And that's what I didn't like about it. So I guess whenever I was turning about 14 or 15, I kind of realized that there is really nothing to believe in... if there's people telling you what to do, and then you see them at the bar, or at their house, doing stuff they're telling you not to do.

"Our pastor, he got caught cheating on his wife with the secretary of the church. One of our secretaries was murdered inside our church, stabbed more than 35 times and raped by three different people in our church. All this stuff is going on. We've had preachers get fired for stealing money. And I just don't see these people trying to tell me what to do. That's why I try to stay away from all that."

Eventually, Lozano says, he rebelled against his parents' attempts to force him to go to church. They pushed back, until the day his mother stopped going.

"My parents were waking me up, and I didn't want to go," he remembers. "There would be an argument, and then I would go. And it got like that until my mom stopped going. Then, I didn't have to go any more. My dad still goes to church to this day, and he still believes that there's a God. My mom still believes that there's a God, a heaven and a hell, the Bible and all that, but she feels that she doesn't have to go to church and worship God constantly."

It was around this time that Lozano developed an interest in what he refers to as 'body art.' He got his first tattoo when he was 15, and now sports a dazzling array of tattoos and piercings that include large silver rings and curved spikes protruding from his eyebrow, lips and chin. Along with his thick, black beard and wide, muscular physique, he presents an impressive, if not imposing sight.

And his appearance, he says, seems to attract people wanting to save his soul. That just reinforces his aversion to anything remotely resembling religion.

"I worked in the mall, and there would be people that would come by and hand me Bibles and little flyers and say, 'You need to find Jesus.' I thought, 'Hey, you're a hypocrite, dude. You're not supposed to judge anybody. How do you know I'm not a Christian already? Just because of the way I look?' Stuff like that is why I don't want to look toward that way. That's one of the biggest things I learned when I was going to church – that you're not supposed to judge anybody. But they do.

"I see the way people are, people that supposedly are Christians, and I don't like the way they act; the way they look at me. I'm not satanic. I'm not trying to draw attention to myself, or make myself stand out. I just like the way it looks. I don't go out to piss people off or shock people. That's not it. This is just how it turned out. It's body art. Just like if you go out and buy a painting because you like the way it looks. This is the way I like to look.

"I walk around and people are trying to preach to me. I'll go to a Christian event with my dad and they'll sit there and preach to me: 'You need to find God.' Well, what for? How do they know that I don't already know this? Which I really do. I've read the Bible at least three times. I know almost everything about the Bible. I went to church for a long time, and I guess the people is what makes me not want to believe in anything. That's why I quit going to church."

One side of spirituality that Lozano does consider is the possibility of spirits, of the dead returning to visit loved ones. He has no idea how that happens, but somehow the idea seems to makes sense.

"I've seen stuff on ghosts and stuff like that, and I think maybe that could happen to some people, but... I don't know, I figure some people do become a spirit, and for some people, it's just closed curtains," he said. "I'd like to figure out what happens when you die. I think you become just a spirit and you're dead. Closed curtains, and it's over. But I really don't think about it too much."

Lozano was born and raised in Midland, a West Texas city of 95,000 on Interstate 20, known as the childhood home of President George W. Bush.

He works now as a successful tattoo artist in the downtown area, and lives with his girlfriend and their two young children. After his distasteful experiences with Christianity, he briefly considered other religions but decided that nothing seemed a good fit. Although he does not expect his religious outlook to ever change, he will not try to influence his children one way or the other. He will encourage them to make up their own minds about spiritual matters.

"My six-year-old, he goes to church with my dad all the time," Lozano says. "He goes and he enjoys it. But I'm not going to make my kids do anything they don't want to do. I love 'em either way. Christian, non-Christian, Catholic... whatever they want to be, that's what they're going to be. I'll tell them my views on it, and give my opinion, but other than that, I will never make them be anything they don't want to be. It's up to them. I'll still love them, no matter what they do.

"Sometimes I do think there is a God, but most of the time I don't. I've checked out some Catholic stuff, but I don't believe in praying to a statue, and telling some man your sins, stuff like that. I've never checked out Buddha, or any of that stuff. I'm not married, because I don't want to get married in a church. I'd like to get married, but not through a preacher. I'd like to get married in a different way, though.

"I have no idea if I'll ever change my mind about God. Like I said, I just live day to day. Whatever happens, happens. Who knows? Maybe there will be somebody who comes along, and it hits me right in the head and makes me look at things a different way. It might happen, but I don't really look toward that."

§ § §

Chapter 12

"It just took a lot of being broken by the world, until I realized, 'OK, this is not all there is, just getting drunk and high. There's got to be something different.'"

A devastating motorcycle crash when he was 19 years old nearly killed Chris Hensley and left him partially paralyzed for life. But even that horrific event failed to slow him down for long.

The self-described "hell-raiser" from El Paso soon continued a non-stop drinking and drugging lifestyle that led to more than a dozen overdoses and a brutal suicide attempt at age 36 in which he swallowed a bottle of pills, drank a fifth of whiskey, then broke the whiskey bottle and used the jagged edge to carve a long, deep gash in his left wrist and forearm.

"Amazingly, I woke up a couple of days later, in my waterbed, in a pool of blood," Hensley recalls. "I crawled next door and had them call 911, and they sent me to the psychiatric center.

"They told me at the psych center that they couldn't let me out, unless they found a place for me (to live). The only place open in town that would let me in was the Christian Home – I'd been thrown out of the rescue missions, Salvation Army, Goodwill, all those places – so I went to this place, and started talking to people there. It didn't take but about 30 minutes before I realized, 'Wow, it's all come around to this; to learning about Christ.' And that's where I was saved."

Hensley, 43, stayed at the facility for three years, taking Bible classes twice a day, working as a volunteer and eventually becoming a staff member. He figures he read the entire Bible "seven or eight times" while he was there, and left in 1999 with a rejuvenated spirit and confidence inspired by his newfound spirituality.

"I was full of the Lord... well, actually, I was full of 'it,' he says, smiling. "I knew that Bible, I tell you, but I still wasn't spiritually grounded. A friend of mine came over one day, pulled out a joint and said, 'Hey, let's get high.' I told him, 'No, I'm with the Lord now; I can't get high.' And I read him a couple of scriptures.

"But he knew the Bible, too, and he said, 'No, no, look here (where it says) I give you every plant and every herb of the field to enjoy, blah, blah, blah.' And it struck me – 'Hey, crazy Joe is right.' So I got high. And then I thought, 'Hey, I'll go to the bars and I'll bring a lot of people to Jesus there.' Before you know it, I fell right back into the hole. But God's grace helped me to get up. So I never actually fell into the hole and stayed, but I certainly wasn't spiritually grounded.

"That lasted about two or three years. Like I said, I wasn't completely fallen, but I know now that I wasn't really saved at that point in my life. I thought I was, but I was really so far from that point... and it wasn't until I started volunteering at the Christian Home again and teaching a class there every Saturday that I truly did become saved."

Hensley, who has lived in El Paso since he was seven years old, was born in Japan, the son of a U.S. Army officer. His mother died when he was a young boy, and his relationship with his father was rocky at best. As he grew, Hensley became increasingly wild and hard to handle.

"I'm sure I was a handful," he says. "My dad was a retired military colonel, and the last thing on his mind was raising a little kid. He didn't neglect me or anything, but we were just very far away from each other. We could be in the same room together, and still be very far apart. I gave him a pretty hard time as a teenager... the psychologists tell me it was (because of) my mom dying when I was so young and this and that, but it was just because, well, I was a very big hell-raiser.

"I had the (motorcycle) accident when I was 19, and that disabled me. I look back on that, and I see that if I hadn't had that accident, I probably would have killed myself in some other way. I was headed right down the road to disaster – drugs, gangs, everything like that. So that slowed me down for awhile, then my daddy died and left me a little bit of inheritance, which I blew in about three or four years. And by that time, I was lost. I had my whiskey bottle, and I didn't know where I was going.

"If you notice, I have a lot of scars on my arm. I would self-mutilate myself when I was drunk, because of the guilt. I knew what I was doing was wrong, so I would cut myself and I would bleed, and

I would be like, 'OK, there you go; you deserved that.' It was like I was getting back at myself for doing wrong."

As a Christian, Hensley believes God is "the creator of the universe." He believes that heaven and hell are very real places, and that the only way to achieve salvation is through belief that Jesus Christ is the son of God, who came to Earth and died on the cross for the sins of mankind.

"From what I've learned in the Bible, the only way into heaven is by God, through his son," Hensley explains. "I believe God is a spirit, and I can't help but picture his son like the pictures I've seen of Jesus. I believe God did come down to Earth in the form of a man, as Jesus Christ, and that's the only picture that I can get of him.

"But even that, it's very distorted, because Jesus probably wasn't even white. I mean, you live out in the desert for so long, you're not going to be a Caucasian-colored person. But in his word, he teaches that we are made from the dust of the Earth, and his spirit breathed life into us.

"If you don't believe in Jesus... there's going to be many who go in front of the Lord and say, 'I did this and that for you,' and he is going to look at them and say, 'I never knew you.' Because either they're not doing it for the right reasons, or they don't believe in him.

"God made man with a free will; he didn't want a bunch of robots. Adam had that choice and he blew it for all of us. He cursed all of us. And because of that, sin has to be paid for. So the Lord Jesus Christ came to Earth and saved us. Through his blood, we are cleansed – if we choose to believe in him. That's the whole trick. We have to believe he is the son of God. And that is the only way we can be saved.

"No one will be excused, because the Bible is everywhere. There will be a few people who will never be testified to or have a chance to look at the Bible, and I'm sure our loving God will take that into consideration. But the sin must be paid for. God hates more than anything to see anybody not be saved, but there are a lot of people who want it both ways: they want to live a nice life and do whatever the heck they want to down here, and then they want to be good with God, too. You can't have it both ways. You have to die to the old self and live for God. There's no middle ground. You can't walk the fence – I've tried it."

Although he has been clean and sober for about a year now, Hensley said he is still tempted at times by the lure of drugs and alcohol. This despite the fact that he was recently diagnosed with Hepatitis C, a potentially fatal liver disease that in all likelihood was caused by his use of intravenous drugs.

"As Paul said, 'What a wretched man am I... stuck in this body of sin.' What can I do, you know? Praise the Lord for his grace, because without that, I would go out there again. I would rationalize my way back out there," Hensley says.

"I get a blood test twice a year, so I caught the Hepatitis C very early, and my liver's still healthy. I did a lot of research on the Internet, and if you live life clean and off the drugs and alcohol, you can go to your 50s and even 60s before it will even start bothering you. My doctor wants me to use Interferon, but there's only a 50-50 chance it will work, and it has a bunch of really bad side effects that I'm not crazy about, so I chose to leave it in the Lord's hands. And I'm going to just use his strength to stay away from the booze and the drugs.

Hensley, who is disabled from his 1991 motorcycle accident, spends four days a week as an office volunteer at Exciting Immanuel church in El Paso, near the Fort Bliss military installation. In his spare time, he reads, dabbles in writing poetry and short stories, and watches "too much" television. Although his life story could be considered a tragedy, he says he tries not to dwell on the mistakes of the past, and looks instead toward a more productive future helping others who are traveling the same roads he once stumbled along.

"I've made it a point not to look back like that," he says. "Because all it was, was a waste. I don't dwell on the past; I just use it as a reference point to learn from. We are saved by the blood of the lamb, and our testimony. I use my past as a testimony, because I can help people by speaking to them. Younger guys who might be going through the same things I went through.

"As I look back on my life, there were so many times I should have died. I shouldn't be sitting here talking to you – a hundred times over – but I praise the Lord that I am. Life is very good. A bit of a struggle sometimes, but the Lord is my shepherd and I shall not want. That's basically how I live. I count on him to help me with everything, and he does."

§ § §

Chapter 13

"I don't use the word God, because the Christians have a trademark on that, and what they mean by it is not what I mean by it."

Tom Davis of Austin has a unique take on the root cause of deadly conflict throughout the history of the world – lack of sex.

"War is essentially people not getting laid," Davis says. "I'm sorry, but it is. When you figure 10 to 20 percent of the men in this society are not getting sex near as often as they need to, that energy has got to go somewhere: football, hockey, war -- aggression."

A former Libertarian Party candidate for the Texas Senate, Davis' theory on the link between sexual frustration and war stems in part from the Wiccan belief system he began investigating and later adopted after returning from a six-month overseas stay in Paris in 1992. Disillusioned with traditional religious teachings, and particularly modern Christianity, the Lake Charles, La., native soon found a strong spiritual connection with paganism.

"I was looking around and had talked to a couple of friends who were Wiccan, and had read some of the stuff, and it just felt right to me," says Davis, who has a bachelor's degree in mathematics from Rice University in Houston, and a master's degree in computer science from Purdue University in West Lafayette, Ind. He spent two years in the Army, and has worked as an assistant college professor, instructor, researcher, computer consultant, systems analyst, and database manager.

"When I have a (Wicca) student, there's always a point when that student will say, 'It feels like I'm coming home.' And if they don't come to that conclusion, they don't belong here," Davis explains, seated comfortably in an overstuffed chair near the front window in his south Austin home. "It just feels like this is right for me. Not that I 'believe' much of anything. It's just a philosophy that makes sense to me, in terms of understanding how things are, and that allows me to organize my feelings about the divine, organize my relationships with other people.

"Paganism is really as much of a life stance as it is a religion, and the people who accept the tenets of Wiccan/Pagan spirituality tend to be people with whom I can relate far more easily. And that's part of it as well."

Davis grew up attending a United Methodist church. Even as a kid, however, he wondered about the doomsday teachings he heard from the pulpit on Sundays.

"I thought it might be possible for a little while, but not for very long," he said. "Jesus says, 'God is love.' Does a God of love drop people into an eternal fire? Hardly. According to Catholic doctrine, most of the world doesn't go to hell, they go to limbo, because they never had a chance to hear about Jesus. Which means they'd just hang around and be bored forever.

"I experienced high school, college disillusionment with what were some obvious lies, fabrications, refusals to even admit there is another version (of truth), other than the accepted one. And I began to realize there are other ways to view the classical Christian scriptures, the classical Christian message. I was a member of a social activist brand of Christianity for quite awhile, and then finally it became obvious to me that Christianity just wasn't speaking to me anymore as a metaphor for the way the universe worked; that it is very involved in masochism, power-tripping... and that's one of the ways the church got so big. The folks who were in it decided they were going to take power, and they did, quite thoroughly. They got Constantine (emperor of Rome from 306 to 337) to say, 'Oh, all right,' and everything else followed.

"Constantine was a pagan emperor for a long time, and on his deathbed he officially converted to Christianity... well, did he really convert, or was that just what the people reported when they came out of the room? But the Roman Empire at that point became officially Christian, and ta-dum."

After a lifetime of searching and study, the 60-year-old Davis answers most questions about God, heaven and hell, life after death and the meaning of life with a consistent, "I don't know." That does not mean he lacks an opinion about those subjects; it is just that he says he does not pretend to have definitive answers.

"I am not arrogant enough to believe that I can understand the universe -- I can't," he says. "Maybe it's a riddle, and our objective is to get as close to it as we can, knowing we can never really get there, and probably would get burned up, if we did. Why are we here? Who knows. Is there a why? There may or may not be. It may be that it's random, but we have a chance to define our own purpose. That's why we have brains.

"Do I believe in God? I don't know. What do you mean by God?

"Human minds are too finite to comprehend anything that even comes close to deserving the word God or divine. I don't use the word God, because the Christians have a trademark on that, and what they mean by it is not what I mean by it. So I usually say, 'the divine.' Does it exist? I don't know. None of us can know. A lot of philosophers have tried to prove that God exists. There's a universe out here, and there are things about that universe that we cannot explain. What caused them? Random chance? Some supreme being? Some group of supreme beings? Aliens?

"I think the only hint people have of something I'll call the divine is something the Christians call the still, small voice within them... that sort of pulls you in a direction outside and beyond yourself. Some people feel it; some people don't. I feel it. So, next question – what is it? How does one approach it? How does one relate to it? What does it want of us, if anything? All good questions.

"So we'll use as a working assumption that there is something that is divine around the universe. If you want to characterize it, feel free. I'm not able to. So what is it? How do we approach it? How do we characterize it?

"Well, essentially, we use the method Jesus used. He used parables to illuminate aspects of it: God is like a mother hen protecting her chicks; God is like the father who welcomes his prodigal son back home; God is like the fellow who, even though he was reviled for being a Samaritan, hauled somebody to an inn and said, 'Take care of it, and I'll pay for it.'

"OK, so we use parables. Now, I think we use parables that speak to us. Not to do that would be kind of foolish. So especially people of European origin use the parables of the old European paganisms, to talk about gods and goddesses – not as if they actually exist, but as a microscope. It brings into focus a small area of the divine very nicely, and fuzzes out all the rest. It's metaphors. You will find people who actually believe in the existence of some of the gods and goddesses; some who use them as metaphor – as I do."

When it comes to heaven and hell, life after death, and whether man has an eternal soul, Davis says he us largely unconcerned about such things. As a pagan, he leans more toward reincarnation as the answer to the afterlife, and says it may indeed be a possibility. The reality, however, as with most everything else in the spiritual realm, remains to be seen.

"There are times that you just want to believe there is something beyond you... either something that caused the pile of shit that you are in, or something that can get you out of it," Davis said. "Maybe there is; maybe there isn't.

"Ultimately, one makes a choice: is the universe benign, malevolent or actively loving? I dunno. I don't see evidence of malevolence, so (it must be) benign at least, and perhaps even a universe that cares what happens, but I don't know. All I know is the people and things around me.

"The Christian church actually believed in reincarnation for a couple hundred years, until the bishops said, 'Uh-uh, that takes our power away. We've got to have enough power that we can tell them they've got to behave this way or they go to hell immediately. We can't let them have another chance at it.' The reason the Christian church got away from reincarnation had absolutely nothing to do with theology. Does reincarnation happen? I don't know. I've talked to a lot of people, and read about a lot of people, who said they had experiences that can't be explained any other way. So it's quite possible. Do we continue after death? I don't know... there's been, with medical science, enough people brought back from 'death' to tell stories, and the stories are all pretty much uniform. I've got to say, well, there's a hell of a lot more evidence for than against. Nobody's come back and said, 'I don't remember anything.' Well, maybe they have and nobody wrote their stories. That's possible.

"If this is all there is, then I'm not going to be around to know that, so it doesn't matter. There's not going to be a consciousness to know that there's no consciousness. Is there a heaven and hell? I don't know. I have around me – everybody has around us – so many people saying, 'You've got to do it my way; you've got to do it my way; you've got to do it my way.' That doesn't make sense, so all I can do is live the best life that I can, which I do anyway, and trust in the universe that what's going to happen next is not going to be horrible. If it is, well, I did my best.

"A quick joke: 'A woman shows up in heaven. St. Peter meets her at the gates and talks to her for a while. 'Oh,' he says, 'you're one of our pagan friends. Come this way.' So instead of going through the big pearly gates, they go around this little garden path around to the side, and they get to this grove where there are people playing, dancing, singing, just having a great time. And he says, 'There you go; join them. That's your group.' And she says, 'But who are those people on the side over there? They're screaming and gnashing their teeth and tearing their hair – what's wrong with them?' St. Peter says, 'Oh, those are the people who believe that pagans shouldn't be in heaven.' The woman says, 'Why can't they just join us? They're in heaven, too.' St. Peter says, 'No, no, no. That's their hell.'

"There are those who says that whatever you believe is going to happen to you, will. You create your own reality. The way it works best for me is that the soul is the part of us that survives this lifetime, and the spirit is that part of us which is who we are in this lifetime. For example, the spirit is inexplicably intertwined with our sexuality; the soul is independent of it. People who report reincarnation report coming back as one gender or the other, and it doesn't much matter. So the difference between those two is just a way of helping people categorize their thoughts on that matter. What will happen to us when we die? I'll find out, but I haven't died yet – not that I know of. I'm in my spirit, not in my soul, at this point. And my spirit doesn't know."

Wiccanism, Davis says, does not involve devil worship, as some believe. He does refer to himself as a witch, and conducts group and individual "rituals" around a homemade altar in his living room. While a five-sided star, or pentagram, figures prominently in such ceremonies, Davis says the idea that such a symbol represents evil is a common misconception.

"Satanists wear the pentagram just like they wear the cross – upside down, as a symbol of disrespect," he says. "It's easy to tell if a cross is right-side up or upside down. Not so with the pentagram. Ultimately, you've got to remember that Satan is a Christian perversion. You've got to believe in Christianity, and take that whole pile to believe in Satan. As far as we're concerned, it's OK, fine, (if) you want to believe that, feel free. Someone once accused the modern founders of Wicca of blaspheming the host – the little cracker the

Catholics use for worship. And he said, 'The term blaspheming the host to us is the same as saying (we are) yelling at a cracker.

"Satan? OK. It's an interesting concept. The real danger in that is that thought forms – entities created by intent of people's will – do exist. And the Christian church may even have created some thought form by their so intensive belief that he be there. And I'm not just talking out of my hat. I've had several interesting situations where a group has gotten together to create a thought form, and it has happened.

"One that comes to the top of my head is... a group in England was meeting, and there was a huge storm, and the lighthouse went out. So they created a thought form, and said we'll create this visualization of a woman and send it out into the ocean to guide the ships. And the people out on the ships saw and actually described what these people had put together (in their minds). So if Satan exists, it's because the church has spent so much energy creating him."

Wiccan worship rituals center around an altar filled with a number of symbols designed to represent the four elements of physics: air, earth, fire, water. After the altar is placed in the center of the room, a spirituality circle is then "cast," as a way of creating a sacred space, Davis explains.

"Once the circle has been cast, you invite in the spirituality of the four elements: earth, representing the body, solidity, groundedness; air, representing mind, clarity, clear-thinking; fire, representing passions; and water, the emotional self, the flow that cleanses you.

"One thing it does is cause us to realize who we are, and what we're about. Essentially, all of the ritual tools have as a main purpose (of) focusing people's attention. Ultimately, we have only one really magical spiritual working tool – the brain. The rest of it helps us focus our attention. A group I was into back in Chicago -- social activist Christianity -- had a ritual that still sort of resonates with me, that began with, 'Let us attend unto our lives, in the name of the father, the son and the holy spirit.' What we are here for is paying attention to our lives. And each other's lives. Being aware of who we are and what we're about, our relationships to each other, ourselves, our community, our world and the divine.

"When you cast a circle and cast it well, something does get created that's not immediately apparent. Two things I've noticed about being in a soundly cast circle: one, you have no desire whatsoever to pay attention to anything outside of it. Not that you couldn't; you just don't want to. And when the circle is taken down, you immediately feel cooler. Because the energy you've contained is in there. There's all kinds of words for it. The New Agers call it subtle energy; chi in Chinese; pri in Hindu. It exists, but we don't have the physical instruments to measure it yet. Have you ever had the experience of someone almost touching you, and you knew they were there? That's the energy I'm talking about. So a well-cast circle holds the energy inside, as well as defining sacred space."

Essentially, Wiccanism is about love, Davis says. Loving and accepting oneself, and one's fellow man. And according to his way of thinking, a return to the 1960s-style philosophy of 'make love, not war' would go a long way toward solving many of the world's problems.

"For Wiccans, the primary rule is 'If it doesn't harm anybody, do what you will.' So (it is) people who are allowing others to do as they will, (and) not violating anyone else's will, and paying far more attention to whether an action harms someone than whether the police are going to throw you in jail. Now, being thrown in jail is to some extent harmful, so if you do something that harms yourself – by getting thrown in jail – then you sort of violated the rule.

"That's why I wear clothes when I go outside. Otherwise, I wouldn't bother. It feels a lot better not to wear clothes, except when it's freezing out there. The Hindus believe that only the purest, most holy people can go around without clothes. You'll see people wandering around the country naked, but they'll say, 'That's a holy man.'

"For us in the United States, nudists – and I count myself one of them – primarily like to do what everybody else does, we just don't like to wear these things," he said, tugging at his T-shirt and shorts. "I always say I wear clothes to keep from getting arrested, fired, fried or frozen. Wiccans will sometimes worship 'sky clad,' which is our word for nude. It's a way of saying we're all equal; it's a way of expressing perfect love and perfect trust – 'I trust you enough that I will let you see my body as it is; I love you enough that I'll accept that body as it is.'

"We believe it's time for us to return sex to its original sacredness: to bring it out of the closet where most people keep it, and recapture its joy and its power. Pagans are pledged to live lives that reflect our dedication to Goddess as well as to God, that are pro-woman as well as pro-man, and that model peace as well as mouthing it. Research has shown that societies that live with open, free, and joyous sex are far more peaceful, happier, and less stressful. Sexually free and happy people are less violent, and more accepting of others."

§ § §

Chapter 14

"In certain aspects, that little spark that keeps us alive is God... so there's a little bit of him in all of us. Kind of like if you take a drop of water out of the ocean – the ocean is God, and we're like a tiny drop of water out of the ocean."

When chronic pain from a work-related injury could not be relieved by traditional medicine, Allen Archer decided to seek help from a massage therapist. To his delight, the ensuing treatments worked and not only soothed his suffering, but also led the Odessa resident into a new career in massage therapy and spiritual healing.

"I was in a terrible amount of pain... and the only thing that was ever able to get me out of pain was a massage therapist," Archer explained. "So I wanted to be able to help people the same way I was helped."

Archer, a native of tiny Buffalo, Oklahoma, worked for 20 years in a pipeline construction business he owned with his father. For the past 10 years, he has worked as a massage therapist in the west Texas town of Odessa. His second career proved a perfect fit, meshing beautifully with his lifelong study and practice of Eastern religion and mystical spirituality.

His interest in non-traditional religious practices first began when he was a young boy, around eight to ten years old, Archer says. He admits it sounds remarkable, but even at that tender age, he began to question the teachings he received at the Baptist church he attended with his parents.

"It was mostly whenever they were telling me that everybody is going to go to hell except for the Baptists," Archer said, laughing softly at the memory. "I was like, 'Ahhhh, that's just not right... God doesn't hate everybody except for the Baptists.' I knew that couldn't be right.

"The whole time I was going to church, I was like, hmmm, they've got some truth here, but it's not all of it. So I just kept trying to discover the whole truth. It just seemed real important to me."

As he grew older, Archer delved deeper and deeper into such things as Buddhism, Hinduism, mysticism. He continued going to church with his family, but spent long hours pursuing religious studies on his own. By the time he was in high school, he admired and began to follow the spiritual pursuits of his favorite musician, the late George Harrison of the Beatles, who was well known for his Hindu beliefs.

"I really studied a lot of what he was into, so that is what probably got me started in it," said Archer, who describes his spiritual philosophy now as an amalgam of Buddhism and Hinduism, with special emphasis placed on intensive daily meditation. "My parents would occasionally find some of the books that I would have, and ask me about them. I would just say, 'Aw, somebody gave them to me, and I was just looking at them.' Needless to say, they wouldn't have understood at all.

"I knew that what I was being taught in church just wasn't right, so I decided I had to figure it out for myself."

He "definitely" believes in God, Archer says, but not the same type of God he learned about back in Sunday school.

"God to me is the all-pervading energy that flows through the universe. He or she is not something you can put a finger on, or even really understand, as far as I can see. I really don't see God as having gender, but I always call him 'he' for some reason. He's more like the spark of energy that keeps us all alive. He's more of that than anything else. In certain aspects, that little spark that keeps us alive is God... so there's a little bit of him in all of us. Kind of like if you take a drop of water out of the ocean – the ocean is God, and we're like a tiny drop of water out of the ocean.

"He's so far beyond our consciousness, beyond our ability to understand him, that nothing we can even imagine can even come close to it. It's something that you just have to believe in, and have love for. The best way to get in touch with (God) is to sit down, remain quiet and just let your mind open up to him. Just meditate, hold your thoughts on him and allow him to come into your heart. That is how you experience God."

Archer says he believes in reincarnation, and so he has no real fear of death. Needless to say, he firmly does not believe in the traditional idea of heaven and hell as places people are sent after their die, depending on certain religious criteria.

"I believe that eventually everyone will get to the point where they merge back into the consciousness of God," he explains. "And that will happen only after you purify yourself by devotion and love, getting rid of any impure emotions – fear, hatred – that block you from reaching your spiritual purity. You do that through meditation, putting your mind on God and keeping it there as much as possible. It's a lot of work, and something that you have to commit to, and do, every day.

"It's a place that everyone eventually gets to... it's just that you have to be woken up to it slowly as you progress. I believe that you are reincarnated many, many times – perhaps millions of times – until you get to that point. If you're here, and you've gotten to this point of being human and being able to know a little bit, you've probably already had a few million incarnations already. So you're getting close, but you've still got a ways to go.

"I don't believe there is such as thing as hell. Whenever there is this void of not having God there, that's where evil exists. A lack of understanding and knowledge of what God is. There's really not an exact thing such as evil, such as the devil and things like that. I don't believe there is a specific evil portion, but it's simply an area where there is a void of the love that exists that is God. It's the fear that maybe someone has more of an understanding of what God is than they do, I think, that really pushes people to an extreme."

Archer does not attend any type of church, but practices his spirituality through self-study and daily meditation sessions, usually lasting about an hour, sometimes more. His work lends itself to spiritual pursuits, as the quiet office where he provides massage therapy is a virtual oasis of calm, peacefulness and serenity tucked amidst the hustle and bustle of the downtown area. Passers-by frequently duck inside the small, softly-lit building for a few moments of tranquility in the middle of their busy day.

Archer says they are more than welcome to do so.

"They can come and sit as long as they like," he says. "I try to do at least an hour of meditation a day. Sometimes it goes into two or three hours, but those are only on the days when other things don't get in the way.

"My meditation has gone to deeper levels. Once you've started with meditation, you learn so much about it. Eventually down the road a little ways, you find someone who knows a little bit more about it, and with a little luck, they'll teach you a little more about it. And the more you go, the more you get to learn. I've been lucky enough to have been taught some pretty amazing ways of meditating. And that's what I do know.

"It seems like the meditator sits and does absolutely nothing, (and) that he tries to escape from the world by doing meditation, but he's not really escaping from the world. He's opening himself up to the real world, which is not anything to do with what you see or feel here."

Along with the massage therapy, Archer also offers "spiritual healing" services, in which he helps people with a variety of physical ailments to re-channel their psychic energy through prayer and meditation, and relieve any number of problems for which medical science has provided them no solution. He figures as much as 70 to 80 percent of common complains for which the average person seeks medical assistance could be relieved through spiritual healing.

"I do believe that doctors do a lot of good, in some respects," Archer says. "There are some things they really help, and then there are some things that they are just there, and God does the healing. They get all the pats on the back, and all they did was... they were just there.

"Most of the time, people come in because they've got a specific problem, some type of ailment – sinus problems, pain -- and nothing has helped. They've gone to the doctors and none of the pills that the doctors have given them has helped, and they've done other things, but nothing has worked. So they try this. I try to help them heal their spiritual body, their spiritual energy. To get it working and flowing best for them. It works."

Archer, who has been married for seven years, says he figures his search for spiritual answers has been an ongoing process covering about 40 years now. His advice to other seekers?

"Keep searching. Keep looking. If you don't find someone who can help you to find what you are looking for, don't be too concerned about it. Even if you don't find it in this life, you'll find it eventually. Just strive as hard as you can to find God within your heart, and center yourself on that one point, and focus on it. If you can do that, you've got everything else made."

§ § §

Chapter 15

"It was just so natural at the time, it didn't even hit me that I was hearing God's voice speak to me. I just answered him. It wasn't until afterward that it dawned on me, 'That was really weird.'"

Longview resident Russell Craft had his future all mapped out. After graduating from the University of Texas with a degree in pharmacy and returning home to go to work, he would one day open his own drug store and eventually build a nationwide chain that would make him rich. When his first store began to turn a profit after only three years in business, he saw his hard work beginning to pay off and his dream becoming reality.

There was only one snag in his scheme.

God had other plans.

It was 1974 and Craft was happily working 90 hours a week at his growing new business. He was married to his high school sweetheart, raising a family and plotting his business empire. Three years earlier, he had decided to rededicate his life to God, after turning away for awhile from his Methodist upbringing while he concentrated on his career. That decision to revitalize his spiritual life came after he heard a stirring testimony during a church service he attended at the invitation of a close friend.

"That just opened a door in my life, and first one thing led to another, then I made a commitment to the Lord," said Craft, who was active in church most of his life, but became less dedicated after he went away to college and started his pharmacy career. "One night about 11 o'clock, I was driving home from a meeting at the church – I remember it was 1971, and I had a little red pickup truck – and as I rode along, I was talking to the Lord.

"I remembered myself being for the first time on a high (diving) board at the swimming pool, and wanting desperately to jump off, but being afraid to do it. You walk out and you look down, then you walk back, and you work up your courage, then you walk back... I felt myself doing that same thing with the Lord. Finally, out of desperation, I just cried out, 'All right, I'm going to do it. I'm going to trust you.' And I felt myself just leap out, and I never hit – he caught me. And my life was instantly changed, instantly.

"I walked in the door that night at my house and my wife was piddling in the kitchen doing something, and she looked at me and she said, 'Something's happened to you. I can see it in your face.' I was never the same again; my life was never the same again," he explained. "My heart was instantly changed. (My) attitudes and actions just began to be foreign to me almost immediately. It was really a strange thing.

"I opened my heart to the Lord and really began to have one of those wonderful growing experiences, where just everything worked. Everything was real and alive, and when I would read the Bible, it was addressed directly to me. It was like everything I read penetrated me, and changed me even more. Like food would do – it changes your body and grows your body – this was happening with my spirit. It was a tremendous experience that went on for months and months. It went on like that for about three years, actually."

Near the end of those three years, Craft says, came a life-altering spiritual experience that he acknowledges "sounds crazy," but is absolutely true. It was during the summer of 1974 that he attended an energetic revival meeting at an Assembly of God church in Tyler, where his sister was a member. The rollicking, raucous service "was the craziest thing I ever saw," Craft says.

"I said out loud to the Lord, 'How can anybody hear anything in the middle of all this noise?' And God said to me – I heard his voice just as clear as a bell -- 'You can hear something. Every word that man says is going to be solid gold to you.'

"Now, I left that place that night, and if my life depended on it, I could not tell you what that evangelist said. But I heard, coming in my own heart, I heard God tell me, 'Go home, sell your drug store, and prepare for ministry.' That man did not say that. But in all that he said, the only thing that I heard was that inner voice telling me to go home, sell my drug store and prepare for ministry.

"Now, I had been to pharmacy school for five years to get that degree, and my vision was to have 100 drug stores coast to coast. And it was happening. My first store had just begun to make a profit after three years, which is very unusual, and we were moving in that direction. I just knew this was really going to be big, and in the middle of all that, he says to sell it. My first response was, 'That's crazy. I can't do that.' And I went through a six-month period – from that summer through January – wrestling with it, and thinking I was going crazy. And everybody else was telling me I was crazy. They said, 'God wouldn't tell you to do that.' My insurance man got so mad at me, he wanted to drop me. People just didn't understand what was going on. People I was in business with thought I'd lost my mind. They said, 'Don't you think you can be a good Christian and help people, and still run a drug store?' I said, 'That's not the issue. This is something he has told me to do, that is going to alter my whole life from here on out."

What made him so sure that God was speaking to him that night, and that he should listen? It was not the first time he had heard that voice. One year before, during a prayer and meditation session at his home with his wife, Craft had a similar experience.

"My wife and I were sitting one morning, praying together in our den, thinking and meditating, reading some together, just listening for God," Craft explained. "Suddenly, I heard a voice speak out loud in that room, just as clear as you can hear my voice right now. I heard that voice say to me, 'If you want to hear my voice, read my word.'

"I had been praying very diligently, 'Lord, I need to hear your voice.' This was when my life was changing so dramatically, and I needed to hear something. It was so odd, and I answered him out loud. And when I answered him out loud, my wife said, 'What did you say?' And I said to her, 'I'm not talking to you.' Then I went quiet again, and he asked me, 'How many books are there in the Bible?' Well, I never had paid any attention, so I said, 'I don't know.' And she said, 'You don't know what?' I said, 'I told you, I'm not talking to you.' So he said to me, 'Well, then turn to the front of the book and count them.' So I turned to the table of contents and counted, and I said, 'Sixty-six.' And then he said to me, 'That's how many ways I'll speak to you, if you'll read my word.'

"It was just like any normal man's voice. It was not a big, booming voice. It was authoritative, and he was in control. He was just very straightforward – 'If you want to hear my voice, read my word.' It was just so natural at the time, it didn't even hit me that I was hearing God's voice speak to me. I just answered him. It wasn't until afterward that it dawned on me that, 'That was really weird.'

"But it was like he just stamped something into me that told me, 'I will talk to you, and you'll be able to understand my ways, if you'll open the book and read it. If you'll really make that the thrust of your life, I'll speak to you every time you read the Bible.'

"What I have learned since then is that I can open the book and read it, and not hear anything from him. It all depends on whether I'm in a listening frame of mind, willing to hear. If it's like, 'Well, I've got to get my reading done today. I've got to be sure I do that,' he is not impressed. He is not impressed with keeping schedules. What he is impressed with is your heart really wanting to hear something. And when I go to him like that, it never fails. I do not hear his voice audibly – I've only heard that voice those two times – but he speaks to me through his word."

Believing in his heart that God was pointing him in a new direction, Craft ignored the skepticism and warnings from his friends and business partners, made that leap of faith and left the pharmacy business for a career in ministry.

He joined a consortium of other Christian men who a short time later founded Longview Christian Fellowship Church, a non-denominational congregation, and attended classes at East Texas Baptist University in Marshall. He led worship for 11 years at the church, then moved to Del Rio for a time to start a sister church in south Texas. Ten years ago, he returned to Longview and has served ever since as pastor for the church he helped organize 30 years ago.

It is a decision the 65-year-old has never regretted.

"I have been around the world to 16 foreign countries, and preached to thousands of people," said Craft, a father of four and grandfather of 18, who has been married for 44 years. "If I were in that drug store today, I would never have gotten out of the drug store. You don't own it; it owns you. You go in there in the morning and you come out at night. If you're not there, the store can't function without that registered pharmacist on duty.

"And I think financially God has blessed me about as much as he would have if I'd been in the store. It's not been for money made, but it's been for things that have happened in my life that have been really good. When I was born again, my life was energized and changed, and when I was filled with the Spirit, I lost my taste for the world. The presence of God, and those times in his presence are what I seek.

"I was with a Sandinista lieutenant in Nicaragua in January – he had become a Christian and we were in a meeting one Saturday morning – and there were about six of us there, praying together. The spirit of the Lord really began to move, and this soldier fell on the floor on his face and began to weep, and he said, 'God, please forgive me; please forgive me.' There was a holiness that came into that little room, (and) I knew that God's presence was there. All of us were changed by that experience. Those kinds of moments are so precious that you would die for those moments. They're holy times, that all the wealth in the world couldn't touch.

"I have no regrets at all. It's been the joy of my life."

While his Christian faith has long been the foundation for his spiritual life, and he believes without question that the Holy Bible contains all the answers to life's most difficult questions, along with the only keys to heaven, Craft says it is wrong for people of one religious faith to denounce those of other faiths.

"Condemnation is not right," he says. "Never should we condemn; we should always love.

"Jesus said, 'I am the way, the truth and the life.' He also said, 'You must be born again.' And being born again is different than belonging to a church; it's different than liking to be around Christian people; it's different than working hard on projects that benefit other people's lives. Those are all good, but it's not being born again.

"You can't continue your old ways... and that doesn't mean you've got to divorce your wife and get rid of your kids. Your heart and your life must change, and Christ must be allowed to dwell inside you. That means he begins to call the shots in your life. That's what it means to be born again. That is how you get to heaven."

As his church and its adjacent kindergarten through 12th grade Christian school continue to grow, Craft says he has a vision for not only his congregation, but all churches throughout the country, to come together and to take a more active role in the community. He wants to see people step outside the walls of their churches and spend more time serving others.

"The church is the people -- it's not the building. And if we're out there, sharing our great faith with people, giving people a word of encouragement, helping them where we can... those kinds of things change people's lives. That's how my life got changed – I heard a man share his testimony.

"I have a vision for the church – not this church alone, but the church of the Lord Jesus Christ – to take its place that the Lord has for it in the community. If you look at our society today, and measure it against society 60 years ago, since the end of World War II... in those 60 years, we have taken the Bible out of schools, we have taken prayer out of the schools, we have made abortion a legal thing where we can kill our own children. And the church has just sat there and let these things happen.

"I don't believe the church should run our society. I don't believe God ever intended that. It's to influence our society. The church's voice is not being heard in the community, and it should be heard.

"There is no outcry against the sin that has taken over our country. And you can't blame the world for that – that's the way of the world. What are people going to do? They're going to sleep together. Why not? If there's nothing wrong with it, why not do it? How are they going to know there's anything wrong with it, if the church keeps its mouth shut – 'Well, we don't want to create any ripples; we don't want to make any waves.' They killed Jesus because of those things. He spoke against it, and they killed him.

"It is a real burden that I have to see the churches in Longview and the pastors of the city come together – not to all say, 'Rubber stamp this; rubber stamp that.' Because we worship differently; we think differently about different things. But there ought to be the foundational understandings that we can all agree to, and we can say, 'This is the right way; this is God's way.' If you don't lift your voice at all, and the only people you preach to is your own people on Sunday morning, what good is that going to do? They're already here.

"My heart is still to see the church become more effective in our world. It's just a weak sister right now, and that just grieves me."

Chapter 16

"I think you are a spiritual being, having a physical experience right now. And you're going to continue to be a spiritual being...I don't think I'm going to die; I don't think any of us do, because you can't destroy energy. That's what we are, energy."

Broken dreams and fickle friends were major factors in Jeri Hyde's disillusionment with her religious upbringing, but those and other traumatic experiences also proved an impetus for a lifelong search that she believes has led her to the ultimate truth.

"I was a little Baptist girl, and I made up my mind when I was about 17 that I was going to become a missionary," Mrs. Hyde explains. "But then I discovered that they didn't have a place for women; they didn't have a place to use us. I was devastated. (They said) well, if you want to become a little Sunday school teacher... this was back in the 1950s.

"Then, I got a divorce when I was in my 20s, after four or five years of marriage, and what I discovered is that people who I thought loved me and supported me were not there at all. They were really embarrassed, and I thought, 'That's not what Christians are supposed to do.'

"I wasn't active in church after that for quite awhile," she said. "I sort of shopped around and looked at different churches and that sort of thing, but I never stopped studying -- reading the Bible and studying other things. I can remember when I was about 20 years old, and I was living in Denver. I had a baby, so I didn't have a whole lot of time to read, but somebody gave me a book. It was a novel, but it had something to do with eastern religion, reincarnation and karma. I will never forget thinking, 'God, don't strike me down.' Because I really was pretty well told that Christian people could not examine that sort of thing. So it must have been the '60s when things started to open up for me."

That first step outside her childhood religion soon led to more intensive study of a variety of faiths, including such things as Hinduism, Buddhism, comparative religions, and Practical

Christianity. During an overseas stay in England, she "church-hopped a lot," looking for something that would be a good fit for her expanding outlook. With her Baptist background still lingering in the shadows of her mind, it was her involvement back home in a non-denominational study group that finally led her to a conception of God and spirituality that made sense.

"I moved back to the States about '75 or '76, and a friend who I knew casually – our husbands had worked for the same company, and they lived in London when we lived there, and in Oklahoma City when we lived there – called me one night and said, 'Jim and I belong to a study group, and we just thought you might like to attend this thing.'

"She said, 'I don't know exactly what your attitudes are, but I just thought you might be interested.' So I said, 'Fine.' And they had just adopted some kids, so I went with her one week and him the next week, so somebody would be home with the babies.

"The first night I went, it was at these people's house, and they played a tape called 'Acres of Diamonds.' And I thought, 'That's super. This is what I want to know more about.' And I was very disappointed, because I was talking to people and telling them, 'OK, I believe this. Now tell me how it works.' And they said they couldn't tell you how it works. They said, 'Well, you can read this book or read that book.' I said, 'No, I want to take a class.'

"Well, we continued to do classes and I read and read until... it's a wonder I have any eyes left. And we finally started a church there, the Church of Religious Science," Mrs. Hyde said.

"One of the things that really came across to me, after all the studying and all the things that I had done, was, 'OK, now it's time to stop studying, and put this into action.' Which really meant taking care of things in my life. I have had experiences where it is just amazing when I can really let go of things and let God handle it. But I seem to have a hard time doing that. Now, I can pray for you, and know that God's taking care of it. Turn loose of it, and it works. It's the times with my own self when I keep meddling, and so it waits and drags on and drags on. It's like my husband tells me: you plant that seed and you say, 'OK, God, I'm going to let you take care of it.' And then you go out and dig it up every night to make sure it's still there.'

"Through my family, we've had deaths, and we took care of my mother with Alzheimer's for years, (and) my husband and I are both cancer survivors. I had a son who committed suicide years ago. Lots and lots of different things have happened that I would not have gotten through without knowing that God was right there, and in charge. I knew I could get through anything, because it's a partnership, and I don't have to beg or make deals with God. That used to be my deal back in my 20s: 'If you'll do so-and-so for me, then I won't ever do this again.'

"It's not a bargaining thing. I don't think God rewards you for your good works, or obviously most of us probably wouldn't have any rewards at all. We are the precious children made in God's image of a loving father, whose great pleasure is to give you the kingdom. And you say, 'OK, what about God's will?' I think God's will is for you to be happy, and as long as whatever you are doing is with a pure heart, and we want things good for everybody else... you can't be selfish with that. It's a constant reminder of how wonderful your life is."

Now living in Plainview, a city of 22,000 in the Texas Panhandle where her husband publishes the local newspaper, Mrs. Hyde commutes 45 miles south to work in Lubbock, home of Texas Tech University, where she serves as a pastoral counselor and pastor for the local Unity Church, a non-traditional religion defined as "practical, positive Christianity."

As a practical Christian, the energetic 70-year-old great-grandmother of two says she believes God "is not only the creator and the source for everything good in our lives, but it is a presence that is with all of us. It is a part of all of us. We're all united. It's the force that runs the world; the energy that runs the world."

"I gave up a long, long time ago thinking of God as that big, white-haired guy in the sky, who marks big Xs next to my name," Mrs. Hyde explains. "I don't think we're being punished for being here. I know that God does not intend for me to be poor and lonely and sick and all of this stuff, if I will just accept the beauty that he has already given me. And so I don't have to die to get my reward.

"There's only one God, and there's only one truth. And I don't care whether it comes from a rabbi or a priest. It doesn't matter. Some people may have to face a certain direction, or light a candle to think that their prayers are answered... and if that's what they believe, it works.

"If you go through the comparative studies, and you look from religion to religion to religion, there's only one truth. Which means that we're put here to love one another; we're put here to support one another, (and) do no harm to anyone else. There is one God, and I don't think God cares whether you call him Joe or whether you call him Susie. It doesn't matter."

She believes there is life after death, Mrs. Hyde says, but not in the traditional Christian sense of a physical resurrection. Heaven, she says, is all around us; hell is self-constructed.

"I think we probably create all the hell that we want to right here. I know I have had some amazing experiences doing that.

"Making a conscious choice to get into maybe a relationship or a marriage or something that you know is going to be so bad for you – and for somebody else. You just devastate one another. What you're doing is... it's like I must be learning something from this. If not, we know that the absolute definition of insanity is to continue doing the same thing over and over again, expecting different results. Some of us take a few times to really keep beating our head against the wall before discovering that it doesn't hurt any more when you quit.

"Every time I've ever gotten myself into a situation where I was just miserable, thank God I could stop and say, 'God, I don't know how to get out of this. Now I'm really going to stop and give it to you this time.' And most of the time, I did. Then you take over again, so you can create another little chaotic situation.

"I saw Billy Graham (interviewed) two or three years ago, and he said he had his idea about what hell was, and he had his idea about what heaven was. And he said, 'I've changed that.' And Charles Gibson, on Good Morning America, said, 'What do you mean, you've changed it?' He seemed shocked, because here's a man who for 50 years has been teaching the same thing. And Billy Graham said, 'Well, it's pretty presumptuous for us to think that we're the only people in the universe. God wouldn't have wasted all this space. And instead of thinking when I die, I'm going to go up and sit on a cloud some place and say, 'Hallelujah, hallelujah,' and strum on a harp, that's wasting our energy. I think there are other jobs for us to have when we leave this body. There's more to do, in different places.'

"We may not understand that, but I think my spirit goes right back into something else. Thank God, because who wants to carry this body around. I think you are a spiritual being, having a physical experience right now. And you're going to continue to be a spiritual being. I believe that whatever the essence is that is you, that spark of life, was created at the same time the world was created. And we probably evolved some way. I don't understand how, but I don't have to.

"Some of the philosophies talk about different levels of paradise. I really think there's something to that. I don't think I'm going to die; I don't think any of us do, because you can't destroy energy. That's what we are, energy. When I leave this body, there is something wonderful out there for me – I believe that. I think we're just going to keep getting better, somehow. I think when we leave, we'll take these troubles, or any problems that we have, with us and we're going to have to learn how to do it all over again. Maybe it's sitting in some other world, who knows?"

Along with that reincarnation-related philosophy, Mrs. Hyde believes that not only is the course of one's life probably predetermined, it is most likely predetermined by each person prior to their own birth.

"I'm pretty well convinced that somewhere along the line I made some kind of a contract that said I'd go through these experiences," she explains. "I really believe that I knew I would do this and this and this, and when I'm ready to go, I can come back to wherever, on the other side.

"I know when my mother was sick with Alzheimer's, I can remember my husband and I sitting there one night and it had just really gotten rough. And I said, 'Why is God letting her go through this?' And then it was like, 'this is crazy.' She didn't have to learn anything through this, but she taught an awful lot of us a lot of lessons. She chose somehow or other to go through it... maybe she chose the wrong raffle ticket, I don't know. But I think she chose to come here and be a stepping stone for some spiritual growth for a lot of people."

Regarding apocalyptic prophecy that warns about the end of the world and second coming of Jesus, Mrs. Hyde again dismisses traditional Biblical teachings. She does not foresee the return of Christ from the heavens, riding on a white steed with a sword coming out of his mouth, as described in the book of Revelations.

"I don't know whether it's going to be a physical thing or not -- I can't imagine Jesus coming down with a sword in his mouth," she said, smiling. "He probably already has (come back)... the spirit of Jesus.

"We keep hearing about the end of the world, and I do believe that is happening. But not everything blowing up and going away. It's going to be the end of the world as we know it, so that a healing has to take place. The rapture, to me, is just something completely foreign. I grew up in the Baptist church listening to sermons all my life, and not one person ever mentioned the rapture, until (apocalyptic Christian author) Hal Lindsey or somebody wrote a book a few years ago. It's the same people who have declared that the world was going to come to an end at such-and-such time, and after two or three times, they get embarrassed and stop talking about it."

To people who are searching for their own spiritual truth, Mrs. Hyde says she tries to follow the example set by Jesus, whom she calls the perfect teacher.

"I say to people, 'Your truth is inside of you.' All I'm here for is to remind you of what you really already know. We need to remind people of how good they are, instead of how bad they are. And that there is nothing that you can't overcome. Look at how many people have been run away from religion. We have these people come in, and they are hurting. They need something, and yet we just scare the hell out of them.

"I think one of the reasons I'm really, really good at my job – and that's not ego; I think I really am good at my job – is because I've never had anybody come in here and tell me anything that shocked me. Because I didn't go from my house as an 18- or 19-year-old child and go into a seminary and come out with all the 'Thou shalt nots.' I got out and I experienced a lot of things, and I threw myself into experiences that were so devastating. And yet, the faith just got stronger and stronger. I should have been dead years ago, but I was so protected.

"Because of all that, I am not going to tell somebody that they're going to hell. I am going to tell them there is a way to work through this. And God knows how to straighten it up, because God didn't make any garbage. It's like you can go back to your mother, and she'll say, 'Well, you know, honey, I wish you hadn't done that, but I'm glad you're here.' I think that's the way it is.

"I think we're here to grow, and make this world a better place. When we change the way we think about life, it changes our life. Whether it's negative or positive. Change your thinking and change your life. Learn to depend on God -- 100 percent -- in every area of your life. Create heaven right where you are.

"That does not mean you're not going to worry about your taxes, and have things to deal with. But if we didn't have things to deal with, that means we'd all still be sitting in a cave some place, wondering how to create fire. God is so good, and things can be so wonderful – when we allow it.

"When you find the truth, you'll know. There's a peace there that passes all understanding. Once you have that, I don't think it ever goes away. It's like blowing up a balloon, then letting the air out. It never goes back into that same little shape it was before. Every time you practice, your faith gets bigger, and you have more assurance of what's going on in the world. And you say, 'Hey, this stuff really works.'"

§ § §

Chapter 17

"When I wake up in the morning, I burn my sage and I give thanks for the sun coming up, the air that fills my lungs, a good night's sleep and pleasant dreams, and for the privilege of walking on the Earth for one more day. I say my prayers to the four directions, asking the spirit of the four directions to guide me today, to be a better person than I was yesterday and the day before."

Jesse "Black Bear" Camacho was raised a Catholic and is still an occasional church-goer, but the 66-year-old retired musician says he feels closer to God when he worships in the spiritual traditions of his Native American ancestors.

"We go to church sometimes, different churches... but when you go to a church, you hear another person preach. You hear another person talk," Camacho says. "When you go into the sweat lodge, everybody has a chance to pray."

Relaxing inside his home and workshop alongside U.S. Highway 287 in Hardeman County, just south of the Texas-Oklahoma border between Vernon and Quanah, Camacho took a break from the handiwork he displays at his Black Bear Trading Co. outpost to discuss his spiritual beliefs. Along with producing a dazzling assortment of handcrafted Indian artifacts, one way he keeps his Aztec-Arapaho heritage alive is by maintaining his forebears' religious practices, including the customary 'sweat.'

To conduct this sacred ceremony, Native Americans gather inside a sweat lodge, a low, dome-shaped structure made out of a framework of willow branches, bent across the four directions – north, south, east and west – and covered with white canvas, representing purity. Other coverings may also be used to ensure total darkness inside the lodge. The sweat lodge in the yard behind Camacho's small frame house is large enough to seat about 15 people.

Rocks are heated in a fire built outside the lodge, then brought inside and placed into a hole dug in the center, where water is then poured onto the red-hot stones to produce steam and superheat the interior.

"Then you begin your prayers," Camacho says. "There are four rounds of prayer – everything is in fours: four seasons, four directions.

"I'm the one that pours the water, so I'm the one who is leading the sweat. Normally, the first round is when you thank God for everything that surrounds you. We're related to everything... anything that lives on this Earth, we are related to. So first, we say a 'thank you' round. Everybody has a chance to do a prayer. When it comes all the way around, we open and close the door, then we start another round. This happens four times.

"The second round is a healing round, where you pray for somebody else. You pray for somebody who really needs prayer – it could be your friend; it could be your enemy. The next round is a blessing round, where you pray that Grandfather (God) will bless me and bless you. When you come out of there, you are very satisfied, because you have had a chance to vent from your heart.

"You come out, you sweat a couple of gallons of water, so you're body has been purified, because you sweat all the toxins out. And your heart is purified, because you speak with your heart and you vent. You pray for yourself and your family; you pray for those who are dying; you pray for those who came before you; and it goes on and on. It's a form of communicating with God. It's something that we do very frequently. You go into the sweat lodge, and you pray for guidance. It's a way to go to church; it's the same thing."

Referring to God as 'Grandfather' is customary throughout various Native American cultures, Camacho says. He also uses the Comanche word for God: 'Nat-tah-meh.'

"Most Native Americans call him grandfather. I was born and raised Catholic, so I believe that same things everybody else believes – that there is one God, and he goes by many names.

"I don't know about today – today is a different world -- but a few years back, when somebody needed advice, help, was in trouble, it was usually easier to go to the grandfather than to go to the father. So the grandfather was a more important figure in any family than the father, the son or anybody else. So out of respect, we call God, grandfather."

His Christian upbringing and Native American heritage give Camacho a true mixed bag of spiritual philosophy. A father of four who has also raised two stepchildren and a younger sister and brother, Camacho's mother was an Arapaho, a tribe well known for its spiritual practices, as well as its association with the Southern Cheyenne, who fought against Lieutenant Colonel George Armstrong Custer in the historic battle at Little Bighorn. In the late 20th century, about 2,000 Arapaho were living on a reservation in Wyoming and more than 3,000 were located in Oklahoma. His father, meanwhile, was three-quarters Aztec, a society that dominated northern Mexico in the early 16th century.

Perhaps fittingly, Camacho lives near the town of Quanah, which is named for Quanah Parker, the last chief of the Comanche, who was known for integrating the Indians' traditional use of peyote – a hallucinogenic cactus plant used by Native Americans in worship ceremonies -- with highly ritualized elements of Christian worship.

"The way the Native American believes -- the way all indigenous people believe -- goes hand in hand with the Bible," Camacho says. "Everything that we believed before there was Christianity, we already believed in those things. Maybe we didn't call them the same things, but we believed in those things.

"The Indian, before Christianity came about -- all those laws and commandments – the male would not have relations with his mother-in-law or sisters-in-law, for example, because of incest. So incest was already in the language of the Native American. When Christianity came, it said the same thing. So, the Bible and the way the Native American believes go hand in hand.

"I believe Jesus was the son of God. Jesus was a good prophet. He is my savior, and the savior of a whole bunch of people. There's a few things that I really am doubtful of... because the people who wrote the Bible, they're humans like you and me. And that was their interpretation of what happened, or what they believed or heard. Jesus Christ wrote very little. He was illiterate. He didn't read or write – he didn't have to. He had the power.

"So there's a few things I'm not too sure about, but I do believe that he sacrificed his life, trying to deliver us from a whole bunch of... shit," Camacho said, smiling. "A lot of people cannot explain who God is. Nobody can. We point to the heavens... God could have been an alien. An alien is somebody who is not from this Earth, (and) God is not from this Earth.

"I do believe there is a heaven and there is a hell. I have spoken to many people of different religions, and there was one person who told me that organized religions are a way to control people, to control their behavior. People tell the little kid, 'If you don't behave, the boogey man is going to come and get you.' The Indian used to tell the little kids that the white man was going to come and take them, because the white man came and took the kids and forced them to go to school. When I was a kid, it was like, 'If you don't behave, the boogey man's going to get you.' Well, the boogey man to the Native American was the white man.

"So heaven could be a make-believe thing; hell could be a make-believe thing. You could be in heaven right here on Earth, and you could be in hell right here on Earth. But being that I was raised Catholic, I believe there are such places as heaven and hell. I do believe there is a good place that we go to, and there could be a very bad, spooky place that we could go to. If a person kills other people, he's going to go to a very bad place. I'm not going to call it hell, but his day is coming when he will have to answer for those things.

"We will be blessed for the good things we do in life. I believe if a person follows the 'red road,' he has very good potential to go to what people call heaven. The red road is a way of life for the Native American. The Hopi calls it 'walking the edge of a knife,' (and) not falling right or left. The straight and narrow. We try to follow that as close as possible."

Ironically, Camacho said, when the white man took control of North America away from the Indians, he violated one of the principles upon which the United States of America was founded – freedom of religion.

"When the Indian was captured, conquered – whatever you want to call it – they were forbidden to do any kind of ceremony that had to do with praising God their way," he explained. "So all of the ceremonials were outlawed. The sweat lodge, not too many years ago, was still outlawed. It was like, 'If you do the sweat lodge, you're going to jail.' It goes back to the Indian not being able to speak their language, to cut their hair, to change their clothing, all of that. They tried to eliminate any kind of religious ceremony that the Indian would have. People thought that when the Indian went into a sweat lodge, they were plotting to overthrow the government or start an uprising, things like that.

"The Indian used to go out in the woods and build their sweat lodge, so that they could do their service. Nowadays, we have the sun dance, which is legal. The sweat lodge is legal now, along with a lot of other ceremonies that were once outlawed. If you think about it, freedom of religion is the reason people came here (to America) in the first place, and then they took that away from the Indian. All the Indian was doing was going in to pray to God."

All those years on the road as a musician and also working as a custom automobile painter left Camacho a humble retirement at best. He depends on income from his small Indian craft business, and spends hours each day painstakingly sewing, carving and building a legacy which would make his ancestors proud. It is a good life, he says, and one that gives him great satisfaction.

"When I wake up in the morning, I burn my sage and I give thanks for the sun coming up, the air that fills my lungs, a good night's sleep and pleasant dreams, and for the privilege of walking on the Earth for one more day. I say my prayers to the four directions, asking the spirit of the four directions to guide me today, to be a better person than I was yesterday and the day before.

"I believe that the purpose of us being here is to live, to live well, without greed or malice. That's what the Hopi says: to live without greed, without malice, and to go forth and succeed in everything you do.

"The purpose of life is to live. Go forth and multiply. Have a baby. The baby grows to be a teenager; the baby grows to be old; and he dies. That is the end of that person. The purpose of living is to live, help others, be a good person. There's one God, and he's got a handle on all this stuff."

Chapter 18

"... I knew that if anything happened to me, I was going to heaven."

Even as deadly machine gun fire sizzled past his head and powerful grenade explosions rocked the desert sands around him, Air Force Staff Sgt. Dan Housley felt an uncanny sense of calm and ease during the heat of the 2003 invasion of Iraq.

That peace of mind, he says, could only have come from one source.

"All my friends and family back in the States were praying for me – there were more people praying for me then than there are now," said Housley, who was among the first wave of U.S. troops to enter Baghdad. "I think my faith in God was stronger over there than it has ever been, and that had a lot to do with the peace I had about me, because I knew that if anything happened to me, I was going to heaven.

"I was scared during the firefights, the ambush... but overall, I really wasn't too worried about it. I was pretty comfortable while we were over there. The whole time we were there, I felt like God was on our side – and I still feel that way. Just the way things have happened, it's obvious that our way of doing things is a lot more spiritual than their way of doing things. Muslims can be very peaceful, but the things these people are doing – beheadings, things like that – are not traditional, not biblical or Koran-based, or anything like that. The stuff they are doing is plain evil, and that's why, in my opinion, God is on the United States' side."

Housley, a 25-year-old native of San Diego, Calif., who graduated from high school in Groveton, Texas, about 90 miles north of Houston, and later attended Texas A&M University before joining the military, was a member of the 15th Air Support Operations Squadron providing "close air support" for the U.S. Army's 3rd Infantry Division during the war. He arrived in Kuwait on Jan. 20, 2003, where he was stationed with the division's 1st Brigade at "Camp Pennsylvania" for two months, before rolling across the border into Iraq on March 20.

As he and his battalion rumbled through the desert toward Baghdad, it wasn't long before the young Christian was using his spiritual strength to help steel his comrades for battle.

"We were the first Humvee to cross the Euphrates River, that far north up toward Baghdad," Housley explained. "Our battalion was the first to do a lot of stuff – the first on Saddam International (Airport); the first to take a palace. The Marines came in from the east of Baghdad; we came in from the west/southwest. We were fortunate to have a lot of tanks and Bradleys (armored fighting vehicles) with us, so the resistance we did face, we mostly just ran over.

"When we were getting ready to cross the river, I mentioned to the other guys, 'I hope you guys are right with God.' We said a quick little prayer or something. They both said, 'Yeah, I'm good.' So we crossed the river and wound up getting into a little gunfight. We finally got down to where we got set up, and the whole night the Iraqis were coming, with RPGs (rocket-propelled grenades), trucks, machine gun fire, stuff like that. We were battling all night.

"Then, the morning we were arriving at the airport... three companies out of the battalion were already there. We were all in Humvees. Now, normally, there's the commander's tank or a Bradley or something with us, but we weren't anticipating any problems along this short little route we were on. All of a sudden, we got caught in an ambush. All these guys in black pajamas came out of this house and ran toward the tree line and started shooting at us. This went on for a good 20-25 minutes.

"We all get out – I had an M-4 (rifle), similar to an M-16 – and we're firing into different sectors. We had two RPGs come really close to us. One blew up right in front of our truck, about 10 feet away. It knocked me back, probably a couple of feet. Then, another one skipped along the ground, underneath our Humvee, underneath the guy's Humvee behind us, and then bounced up, hit him in the chest and bounced back on the ground. It just cut his thumb; it didn't blow up. We were just kind of standing there in awe. Finally, the fire died down in the tree line."

Housley went on to spend a total of nearly four months in the Middle East before arriving back at Fort Stewart, Ga., on May 4. After five years on active duty, he now serves part-time as a member of the Air National Guard's 165th Air Support Operations Squadron, devoting one weekend a month to military service while attending college and pursuing a master's degree in business.

He hopes to eventually earn that degree from Texas A&M, where he spent less than a year after graduating from high school. A painful breakup with his high school sweetheart led to his dropping out of school during his second semester and picking up a hard-partying lifestyle that caused him to turn away from a strong religious upbringing that lasted throughout his childhood.

"We met at church during my junior year in high school, and God was always pretty much the center part of our relationship, but by the time we went to college, God wasn't even an issue in our relationship, and that tore us apart," Housley says, of the split that broke his heart. "I was pretty much crushed, and couldn't really go on with school. I tried for another month or two, but I just couldn't do it."

Despondent and looking for a new direction, Housley joined the Air Force and entered a phase of his life he refers to as the "dark times." Several years of continuous boozing and carousing with fellow soldiers at Fort Stewart, mixed with regular pangs of conscious and tugs from his pious past left him at a crossroads during early 2002.

"I had been drinking a lot, going nowhere, and I knew something was missing," he says. "I knew I needed to get back to church.

"Even when I was in those dark times, there were times me and my friends would start talking about Jesus. As a matter of fact, one of the last parties I went to, I told everybody, 'Look guys, I can't do this anymore. I've got to get back in church, and get my life right with God.' This one guy -- a friend of mine who I haven't hung out with since – gave me his number as I was leaving and said, 'Make sure you call me. I want you to invite me to church.' He never came, and he's still not doing too well."

His first move to straighten out his life, Housley says, was to check himself in to a military alcohol and drug abuse program, a somewhat unusual decision, since most soldiers who wind up in the program are ordered to attend. A subsequent evaluation of his drinking patterns indicated he had a serious alcohol problem, but Housley says he quickly discovered that what he really needed was to rededicate himself to his faith.

"It was a good course, but all it really did for me was tell me that I needed to get back to church. It wasn't that hard to stop drinking –

there were no withdrawals or anything like that. It was just that I had to find something else to do.

"Some of the things they tell you when you're in the program... the signs of an alcoholic are: do you drink alone, more than one night a week, are you blacking out when you drink? I fell under every category they had, so I thought I was an alcoholic. But I just stopped. If I wanted to drink a glass of wine or something now, I could drink it. No problem. It's not like the next day, I would just start boozing.

"When I left my old life behind me, the hardest part of it was all the friends I had in the military. I still saw them on a daily basis. The work I do... it's an all-male, combat career field, so the testosterone level is sky high. If you think of the worst possible locker room in the world to be in, that's it. So it's really difficult – not laughing at certain jokes, things like that. It's harder when I'm with them than when I'm not.

"But they've all seen a change, because they'll say things like, 'You can't do that in front of Housley; you'll go to hell.' So I think I made somewhat of an impact, but I don't know. I've had my ups and downs, but more ups than downs. Eventually, I hope to just be on a steady uptrack."

Housley has come full circle with his religious beliefs, from a devout youngster active in his church youth group to a devoted family man who holds hands with his fiancé in the midst of a crowded, noisy restaurant and prays over his noonday meal. He still struggles at times with various hardships the world has to offer, but with so much good fortune in his life and exciting prospects for the future, he has no doubt that a higher power is watching over him.

"God has been extremely merciful on me," he says. "There were times when I was on active duty, just doing things I shouldn't have been doing – partying – and he's still allowed me to do well in the military, progress much faster than most people do. He helped me to meet a wonderful Christian girl...

"I think the reason God was merciful to me is because even during those times I was doing bad things, I felt guilty. I had the Holy Spirit with me. At certain times, I think I felt the Holy Spirit leave me, because I was going completely against God, but for the most part, it stayed with me. When you do something wrong, you feel bad – and that's the Holy Spirit, that little voice inside, saying, 'You shouldn't be doing this.'

"I believe everything the Bible says. I believe I'll never fully understand it, no matter how many years I've read and studied it, but I don't think any man will ever understand God's true purpose. It's just too awesome, too great.

"I kind of think of the Bible as a rule book – everything we're supposed to do is right there. The Bible says we're all sinners, so we're not necessarily going to do right all the time, but that's why we have Jesus. He died for us on the cross, (and) rose for our sins.

"It has a lot to do with how I was raised, but also just through prayer. Especially over the past five or six years, I've seen God work in my life in ways that has brought realism to it. Stuff that I've prayed for, and the way things have lined up in my life. It's just given me more faith. And that's the biggest key to believe in any of it – just faith. How many other men in the history of the world have been able to make an impact like Jesus did? Everybody in the world pretty much knows about Jesus. If he was just another man, a really good guy walking the streets of Jerusalem ... if he hadn't performed all those miracles, and all that other stuff didn't really happen, you wouldn't see an impact 2,000 years later.

"A lot of stuff in Revelations is starting to come true, but I don't think this is the end times. I think our measurement of time is so far off, according to the Bible. I believe in my lifetime I will experience a lot of the hardships the Bible talks about, but I don't think... I would love for it to happen, but I don't believe Jesus is going to come back in our lifetime."

§ § §

Chapter 19

"I was walking across the street to my truck, and I told the Lord that my life was his."

It was an unusually bright East Texas evening sky 12 years ago when Jerome Denmon walked out of a weekend gospel music concert in Gladewater and saw what he considered a sign from heaven.

"It was at this old theater, and this group that was singing did a lot of testimonies, and they answered a lot of the questions I'd always had," Denmon recalls. "One question I had was why in the world anyone would want to sing gospel music, when they could sing rock and roll, and make a lot more money. And this guy answered that question.

"He told me that night that he was singing for the Lord. He had chances to sing with popular singers, but he chose to sing for the Lord. One guy, he had a crippled hand, and he said that one day he would have two good hands. They gave me an invitation to come down to where they were (for an altar call at the front of the auditorium). I wanted to go down, but the devil was telling me that I would look stupid, (and) that I was already saved, so there was no sense in going down there. So I didn't go.

"Then, when I walked out the door that night, I looked up in the sky and it was the prettiest sky I'd ever seen in my life. My wife was with me, and I told her, 'What a beautiful night it is.' I guess it was a full moon that night – I don't remember – but it was real blue and had a lot of white clouds, and every cloud looked like an angel. When I saw that, I knew I was saved," Denmon says. "I was walking across the street to my truck, and I told the Lord that my life was his. If he could forgive me for everything I had done, my life was his.

"I thought I was a Christian all my life, because I knew there was a God. But I never really gave my heart to it until that night. I was already going to church at the time, but I went because I thought I was supposed to. I went and talked to my pastor and told him about my experience, and he said, 'Well, it sounds to me like you got saved.'
"

Since then, the 60-year-old DeKalb native has dedicated his life to serving God, his family and his Missionary Baptist church. Along with his work as a barber in downtown Kilgore, he has served more than seven years as church Sunday school director, and also been ordained as a deacon and begun to preach occasional sermons.

He was never "a real bad guy," Denmon says, but his life has changed in significant ways since he prayed that night for salvation.

"I never have been in jail or anything like that," he explained. "I did drink beer once in awhile, stuff like that. But I haven't touched one since then. I just started looking at things different. Used to, I didn't have time to go to church – I'd rather go fishing. After I became a Christian, I sold my boat. I don't have time to fish any more. My free time is (spent) working for Jesus."

Denmon, who has a daughter, two stepchildren and seven grandchildren, is a 1961 graduate of Sabine High School in Liberty City, a town of about 1,600 people just outside Kilgore, home of Kilgore College and the world-famous Kilgore Rangerettes drill team, founded in 1940 by the late Gussie Nell Davis to perform during football halftime periods. The Rangerettes are known as the first precision dance team in the country to perform on a football field, and as the inspiration for creation several years later of the famed Apache Belles drill team at nearby Tyler Junior College.

After spending four years in the military following high school, Denmon earned his barber's license, and has spent the past 33 years cutting hair in the same small shop in downtown Kilgore, a bustling town 120 miles east of Dallas where the streets are decorated with small replicas of oil derricks, and the population has grown since 1970 from 9,495 people to an estimated 11,339.

The city may have gotten larger, but not a lot about the downtown area has changed, Denmon says, explaining that he has had many of the same customers visiting his barbershop since 1971. Some of those customers follow faiths different from his, but Denmon says that he believes there is only one way to reach heaven.

"I don't have no quarrels with anybody else's religion, but if they don't believe in Jesus, I believe they're going to go to hell. I sure do," he said. "The Bible tells you that the only way to heaven is through Jesus. So if you believe in the Bible, you believe that way. There may be (another way), but I'm not going to take that chance.

"There's a lot of answers I don't know, but I just know what I believe. We're here on this Earth to witness for God, to tell people about Jesus. The last two verses in Matthew will tell you that.

"I can't tell you why Jesus hasn't come back yet, but he's going to come back. Why he hasn't already done it, I don't know. But I believe he is coming back, and when he does, there is going to be a lot of disappointed people. There are a lot of people in this world who think they're Christians right now, but they're not. They believe, like I used to... they know there's a God, but they know it in their head, and not in their heart. If you don't know it in your heart, I don't believe you're a Christian."

Being a follower of Jesus Christ has given Denmon peace of mind, and a comfort in knowing that not only is his soul going to spend eternity in heaven, but also that God is in charge of his life, and that whatever troubles may befall him, there is a divine reason for everything that happens.

"How do I know that? That's a hard question to answer... I'm not sure I can put it in words," he said. "You can just look around and tell there's a God.

"I've had a lot of bad luck since I became a Christian, but nothing has ever shattered my faith," he said. "I had a great-grandson who was killed when he was two years old, in a car wreck. It was hard, but I knew there was a reason for it. And I don't blame God for it. He doesn't control our actions. We're not robots. If he wanted to, he could make us all Christians, but he's not going to do that. It's got to be our choice. What we do is our choice. You just have to believe. You may not ever know the reason why something like that happens, until you get to heaven and ask God.

"Just because you become a Christian doesn't mean your life is going to be a bed of roses. Bad things happened to Jesus. You're going to have trials and tribulations. I don't know why bad

things happen to good people, but I know there's a reason for it. And some day, I 'll know the answer."

§ § §

Chapter 20

"When I was a kid, I was raised in a Pentecostal church... it wasn't an option. I tell everybody I had a 'drug problem' – my grandmother and my mother drug me to church."

Witnessing the birth of his daughter 20 years ago was enough to convince Monahans native Roy Bean not only of the existence of a higher power, but also that it was time for him to return to his Christian roots and make God a more central part of his life.

"That was really an eye-opening experience for me," Bean says. "I was in the delivery room, and they had to do a C-section, so that was a little bit more than I probably bargained for. But it was a turning point in my life – realizing that life was a gift, and that a child is a gift from God.

"Just seeing human life being born, that really solidified it for me. To know that I didn't crawl out of the sea, or out of the ground as an amoeba, and then evolved.

"I'd been exposed to the Bible and heard different preachers, so the Gospel had been shared with me all my life. But just stopping and looking at the bigger picture, instead of just myself, and looking at the world... there again, a baby being born into the world, I don't think that's an accident. I don't think that evolution had anything to do with that. What the Bible tells me is that I am made from the dust, created by God. I sure don't believe that I came from apes."

Bean, a 44-year-old father of two, has lived all his life in Monahans, a town of nearly 8,000 people located 36 miles southwest of Odessa, in the heart of cattle and oil country in northeast Ward County. Despite his West Texas heritage, he is not named after the legendary Judge Roy Bean (1827-1903), a self-appointed justice of the peace who called himself the "Law West of the Pecos," and held court sessions and dispensed his own unique brand of Texas frontier justice in his saloon along the Rio Grande River, in a desolate stretch of the Chihuahuan desert.

A longtime natural gas plant worker, Bean got married when he was 21 years old, and became a father three years later. He had stopped attending church as a teenager, but never really gave up on his faith. He enjoyed going to bars and shooting pool with his friends, but he was not a heavy drinker and so had no trouble turning his back on the neon lights when he decided to devote his life to his religion and his family.

"It was in 1985; I was 23," Bean said, sitting at a conference table on the second floor of First Baptist Church of Monahans. "There was a crowd that I hung with, and a lot of them today have turned away from that life, but there's still some that haven't given up that nightlife yet. As a matter of fact, last weekend we went to Lubbock for my wife's 25-year class reunion. And I seen some of my old buddies and everything, and they're still drinking... it was hard enough for me just staying up past 10 o'clock.

"Anyway, we had a small child at that time – she was just six or eight months old, maybe. And I had a guy who was coming by the house now and then, witnessing to me about Christ. And he always would tell me the same story. He was an older gentleman, and he would say, 'Well, if you believe you come from apes, I just have one question. Where did the apes come from?' He was joking, but he wasn't.

"I just felt that it was something I needed to do, to make sure I was right with my creator. I didn't like what I thought would be the other path, so when the fellow came into my home this time, we were discussing Christ and I asked him if he would pray with me. I asked Jesus to come into my heart and save me... and I've known a peace about it ever since the day that I done that."

While he says he lives each day with doubts and unanswered questions like anybody else, Bean says his spiritual faith and foundation is rock-solid. He believes unwaveringly in the words of the Bible, that there definitely is life after death, and that there absolutely is only one way to enter heaven.

"I do believe Jesus came to this Earth and walked on this Earth for 33 years. I do believe that once saved, always saved, because he died one time on the cross for all of mankind's sins," Bean says. "There again, I go back to the Bible.

"My Bible tells me that no man comes to the father unless it's through Jesus Christ. A lot of things are open to interpretation, but all I can say to someone is that if you believe that Jesus Christ died on the cross for every man's sin, then you believe in Jesus Christ.

And if you profess him as your Lord and savior, I believe you'll go to heaven. I believe that's the only way to get to heaven. I'm not going to knock another religion, because it's each individual's prerogative to believe what they believe. If somebody can show me something different, I'm more than willing to sit down and listen to them. But I don't know that I'm going to change my mind."

Bean says that although he doesn't claim to understand it all, his faith in God has been reinforced a number of times during his life, but a pair of back-to-back brushes with serious injury and possible death provide a personal illustration of what he believes was divine intervention. He believes God is in charge of the universe, and that everything that happens here on Earth happens for a reason. Why bad things happen to good people is one of those questions for which there is no easy answer, he says.

"I know God allows things to happen, for a reason," Bean said. "Looking at the bigger picture... let's say the individuals that get blown up in a car bomb. I don't know their status, I guess. I don't know if someone else may come to know Christ because of what happened. I don't know why he would allow kids to be killed, or somebody to live and somebody else not to live. I just don't know. I just have to go back to the Bible on that, and that's all I can tell you. The good book tells us that we won't know every answer to every question, so it's back to faith.

"In 1987, I was working at a natural gas plant. Our process consisted of taking gas at 5 psi (pounds of pressure per square inch) and compressing it to somewhere around 800 psi. I was working at a compressor station, and a compressor cap blew off in my face with 780 pounds of pressure. I was wearing a hard hat, but no safety glasses, no flame-retardant clothing. Those things were recommended at that time, but they weren't required.

"It burnt my eyes... like a welding burn. Basically, they hurt open (and) they hurt closed, but I wasn't blinded. My vision wasn't even permanently damaged. Less than a year after that, I had a car battery blow up in my face. I was wearing a green satin John Deere jacket, and it was just speckled (from being splashed with battery acid). Other than that, I was OK.

"I always said both of those incidents were wake-up calls. That compressor that had that cap blow off... that machine was compressing gas, and the volume that it pumps is like a million-and-a-half cubic feet per day. Well, you've got a 4-inch opening, with 750 pounds coming out of it, with an open ignition system. There were any number of points that it could have lit. If it had, I would have been (engulfed) in a ball of fire. But it never did catch on fire.

"I believe God had something to do with that. I believe in divine intervention, and I also believe that everything happens for a purpose. I believe in faith. That's what sustains me, knowing in my heart from reading the scripture and studying the word that I am a sinner, but I am saved through grace."

Having faith in something one cannot see is a difficult thing to explain, Bean says. He compares it to the emotion of love, or even the air we breathe. What it finally all comes down to is a matter of choice, making a decision.

"It's really for the individual to decide. You'll stand before God in judgment; I'll stand before God in judgment. I would rather err on the plus side than on the minus side. If I'm wrong, so be it. When I die, my body goes back to the soil. But if I'm right, then I get to reign in heaven with Christ.

"If I'm wrong, then I've treated people the way I want to be treated. And I don't have to worry about hurting someone's feelings intentionally. I've got a conscience. Everybody's got a conscience. I've seen what some people do... what I would call evil. I don't believe in treating another individual in any manner that will harm them, demean them, degrade them, whatever.

"I've got a (cemetery monument) business here in town. I deal with grief-stricken folks pretty regular. When I deal with them, it's in a time of grief and sorrow, and a lot of people wait a period of time before they make any type of decision. And then I have people who come to me in less than a week, and money is no object to them. They don't care. I dealt with a couple of ladies about two months ago, and money was no object. They wanted the biggest, the best, and they wanted everything on this monument. And what normally would have been a $700 monument, they had taken it to $1,700.

"I didn't have the heart to tell them that I would do that. I just told them, 'Ladies, y'all need to take some time and grieve. You want to honor your mother, and I understand that. But don't make a decision now.' I could have gone ahead and taken advantage and said, 'Sure, we can put all that on there.' But I felt good about what we ended up with after the final decision, and it wasn't anywhere close to what they wanted originally."

To anyone who is out there searching for answers, seeking spiritual guidance, Bean recommends the path he has chosen. It is a simple exercise, he says, involving prayer, commitment and study.

"Salvation's easy; it's one of the easiest things there is to do. All you have to do is ask Jesus to come into your heart and live, and abide in you. And there are some changes that will take place. It's not something that will happen overnight, but if you read the word and study the word, that's the road map as far as what you should and shouldn't do. It's like anything else; it doesn't just automatically happen. But at the same time, you've got a choice. And you'll know if it's right or wrong.

"The guys out at the plant, they're always talking about holy rollers and all this, you know. I just tell them, 'Hey guys, you know... if I'm wrong, then I'm just dead. But if I'm right, then somebody else is going to have to stand there and answer the questions.' I feel like you've got to lead by example. I'm not perfect – I stumble every day. There's things that I say and do that are wrong, but all I can do is the best that I'm able to do, and realize that I am human and not beat myself up. I've just got to try to do better."

§ § §

Chapter 21

"The significance of life for me is the joy in living it."

"When I open myself up to everything that I am feeling – the sadness of having lost something, the tremendous embarrassment of having said something – when you get to that depth, that much openness, God is waiting for you inside of that."

Take one recovering Catholic, add a dash of Baptist theology and a splash of Methodism, mix thoroughly with liberal doses of Buddhism, Hinduism and existentialism, then stir in a healthy measure of Carl Jung psychology and what do you have?

Julie Palmer.

Mrs. Palmer, a Houstonian who was born in Venezuela, is a seeker, a scholar, a student, a teacher, mother, wife, daughter, dreamer, thinker, intellectual and philosopher, who has spent much of her adult life searching for answers to some of mankind's most fundamental questions -- what is the meaning of life? Who is God? Why are we here, and where are we going?

After decades of exploration, extensive studying and intensive self-examination, the 50-something mother of four says she only recently found what she has been looking for all her life.

"The goal of life is not to be perfect -- it's to be complete," Mrs. Palmer says. "It's to be exactly who you are. That's what I'm all about.

"When I open myself up to everything that I am feeling – the sadness of having lost something, the tremendous embarrassment of having said something – when you get to that depth, that much openness, God is waiting for you inside of that. And the reason I know that is because of the tremendous feeling of grace that I get when I do that. Even when you face something bad in yourself, that you have not wanted to admit -- when you do, it hurts like crazy and you feel like the worm of the world, but when it's all over, there's unbelievable grace, because you have accepted a part of yourself that you always had hidden in your psychic basement. And this grace is just like they talk about in the Bible – it's ecstatic.

"God, to me, is this tremendous loving energy that is in all of existence. And it's a very real thing. Every single one of us is a manifestation of this divine energy, and the more we know about ourselves, the more we get to that central core in each one of us. And when you look deep enough inside yourself, you're going to find God there waiting for you.

"Whatever our purpose is, we are supposed to be who we are, and really and truly be it," she said. "God wants you to be not the best that you can be, but all that you can be. So wholeness is the goal, not perfection."

Born in Venezuela in 1946, Mrs. Palmer was nine years old when she and her family moved to the United States. She was raised in the Catholic church by an agnostic father and a mother she describes as a "very spiritual person" who grew up in an orphanage run by nuns, but did not attend church services regularly. Even as a child, though, she began to question her religious teachings.

"I was still in Venezuela when I did my first communion, and it was very difficult for me... because I didn't believe anything they told me in catechism class," Mrs. Palmer said, smiling at the memory. "I must have picked up my father's skepticism somehow."

She stopped going to church at age 15, and soon discovered an affinity for history and literature. Her closest friend in high school introduced her "to everything that has been important in my life since," including music, philosophy, the world of counter-culture and most importantly, the teachings of Carl Jung, the famed Swiss-German psychoanalyst.

After getting married in 1970, Mrs. Palmer moved to England with her new husband, where she quickly experienced a crippling sense of loneliness, separated for the first time from her family and friends. In trying to better understand and make sense of her feelings, she happened upon a book written by Jung, "Man and His Symbols," which seeks to explain in layman's terms such psychological concepts as the importance of symbols in the unconscious mind, and the interpretation of dreams.

"The minute I opened that book, I knew I had found something really significant," Mrs. Palmer says. "I read that book in a few days, and was just feeling like I had found paradise. So many answers to so many questions that had eluded me.

"The world literally got put into place when I read Jung. The thing he says that is so important is that life has both light and dark in it – and so do we. And we make a tremendous mistake when we identify only with the light, and push away all the dark. You do not banish the dark side – it just comes and gets you from behind. We all know of the preacher who is a monster to his family, or the preacher who gets caught in the hotel room with some lady of the evening. The answer is to see the darkness in oneself, and make our peace with it."

Her first marriage eventually ended in divorce, and Mrs. Palmer went through a self-described "hedonistic" phase -- party, party, party -- that ended several years later when she met her second husband and became a Baptist. She faithfully attended church for three-and-a-half years, but became disillusioned after realizing "the tremendous disparity between what Jesus said and what Christians do." Her beliefs were further complicated by a decision to seek counseling, and undergo her first Jungian psychoanalysis sessions.

"I always had this natural belief in the goodness of life, and in the fact that there was God. And I could never really shake that," she explains. "During this time was the closest I came to accepting the whole (Christian) ball of wax. I tried for a long time, and I was very committed to it. I started really reading the Bible, and I liked all the stuff Jesus said, and I didn't have any trouble putting those things together with the things Jung was talking about, but I had all kinds of problems with Christianity and all their limitations. I had already read about Buddhism, Hinduism and Zen, so I had been around the block too much to accommodate this narrow view.

"I think that the world is made up of people who have to control everything, and of people who are more like – 'Well, let's see what life brings us.' More in the flow, and willing to live with ambiguity. I really think that is the bottom line – that many people simply cannot live with ambiguity. They have to have everything very definite, no gray areas... and then they get very rigid and inhuman. I think that is the problem with fundamentalist anything. It is scary, because it is unforgiving. You can't be human and be unforgiving.

"My favorite thing I found out was, when Jesus was asked what is the greatest commandment, and he says it is to love the Lord God with all thy soul, with all thy heart and with all thy strength. And the second greatest commandment is to love your fellow human being the same way. But at the same time, I thought, this religion is not what's really being done here. It just got harder and harder to accept."

After leaving the Baptist church, she returned to her studies at the Jung Center in the Montrose area near downtown Houston. She concentrated her spiritual energies for a time toward her work as a hospital maternity nurse and to the raising of her children. Along the way, she also spent three years as a member of a local Unity church, made up basically of Christians who believe in reincarnation, before once again becoming disenchanted with organized religion and going "churchless for a long time."

"I had no problem with Jesus," she says. "Jesus was very cool. But I couldn't handle his churches."

Finally, after undergoing "an awakening of sorts" while watching the 1982 movie, "Ghandi," when she was 36, Mrs. Palmer experienced a dramatic, life-changing epiphany she refers to as a "conversion experience." It all began with a simple walk around the block with her analyst, a former Methodist minister who asked if she wanted to join him while he smoked a cigarette prior to a counseling session.

"I asked him, 'What do you think about the Resurrection (of Jesus)?'

"He says, 'I get to listen to an awful lot of people talk about an awful lot of things that they would never say outside. And when people die -- when people have loved ones die -- it is amazing how many times they have some sort of manifestation (visit) from that loved one after they're dead.' He said he has had them himself. He said, 'I know it is true, so it doesn't surprise me in the least that someone as spiritually adept as Jesus would come back after he was dead, and appear to his friends and his family. I don't think he was resurrected in the body, but I think he appeared to them.'

"That whole thing made the whole Jesus problem approachable for me. So I went and I got John Crossan's book on the historical Jesus, and then I fell in love with the historical Jesus and began to study him, and really got to see him in a depth I'd never seen him."

A short time later, after reading an article on Christianity written by professor Huston Smith, a series of vivid dreams proved to crystallize Mrs. Palmer's religious beliefs and pave the spiritual direction for her life:

"The next morning, I dreamt I was in Galilee with Jesus and two other male apostles. And we were walking in the desert -- with a whole bunch of other people, too -- and Jesus motions to us and we go behind these great big monolith-like rocks. And he stands and he opens his arms, and his heart is this energy sphere that I can see. And it literally comes out of his chest and gets bigger and bigger and bigger, until it encompasses all of us. And we all get this marvelous, loving feeling. And then I see that the same thing is happening to us, that our hearts are growing and encompassing the other three. And I think to myself, 'Oh, this must be the trans-substantiation' (doctrine held by Roman Catholics in which the bread and wine in the Mass is converted into the body and blood of Christ).

"Then the alarm rings, I hit the snooze bar, I go back to sleep and have the exact same dream all over again, which I never do – maybe once, twice before, I have had repeat dreams. And again I say, 'Oh, this must be the trans-substantiation.' The alarm rings again, I whack it again, go back to sleep, (and) have the same dream again, except this time Jesus is transparent from the waist down, and I know that he has died. Which is a direct answer to the question that had started this whole thing."

Later that day, she is in her analyst's office, relating the dreams to him.

"As I start to tell him the dream, the same thing is happening to me as happened in the dream," she says, pausing to compose herself as her voice chokes with emotion and tears fill her eyes. "This is difficult for me to talk about... I can feel my heart expanding, and Henry (her analyst) is sitting right across from me, and I can tell that he is getting it as well. Because as I tell him the story, we start getting that energy, and then I go into the second part of the dream and it's getting hard for me to talk, and then I literally felt the energy go right into my head, and he said, 'Oh, I felt it, too.' It's like we had this third energy in the room with us, and it filled the entire room. And I couldn't talk anymore.

"Then when I calmed down enough, I said something like, 'And now, I want to follow Jesus.' And we both burst out laughing. Because it's such a Jesus freak thing to say, and I couldn't believe I was saying this. But I meant it – and that was what made it so funny. I was laughing, and I had tears streaming down my face. And we stayed in this beautiful, powerful state with this third entity –

whatever it was – for the rest of the session, which must have been another 40 minutes."

After the session, she went to lunch with her husband, told him the story, then spent the rest of the afternoon in the neighborhood Catholic church, meditating and thinking about the whole experience. Once again, she tried attending regular church services – the Catholic church this time -- but lasted only eight months.

"It was just too small, too confining," she said. "I don't like a guy up there in skirts telling me that women can't be pretty."

Now, Mrs. Palmer is an active member of the Unitarian Fellowship of Houston, a liberal "free religion" church that welcomes believers and non-believers of any and all faiths, including Jewish, Christian, Buddhist, naturist, atheist and agnostic. This tolerance and even celebration of widely-varying individual beliefs makes it a perfect fit for someone who calls herself a "very modern Christian."

"I am definitely a Christian, because of the experience I had – the dreams. But the thing with me is that Jesus is most definitely the son of God, but so am I. Only he is really good at it, and he came back to tell us about it," she says, laughing.

"He is the same kind of person Buddha is... I think Gandhi is that same kind of person. I don't

know if he's as huge as Jesus was, but Gandhi was able to stop -- several times while he was there -- stop people from killing each other. He was able to bring about this spiritual human dimension that actually got all kinds of people to get on the same wavelength with him and work for peace, rather than for killing one another.

"The Bible is a great book -- but it's only one of God's sets of words. And it's God's words coming through human microphones. So it's going to have only part of the picture.

"It's like the story of the elephant and the four blind men: one feels the tail and says, oh, this animal is very skinny and thin; then another feels the ears and says, no, it's very broad and it flaps; and another one feels the foot and says, no, it's big and wide and strong. They're all right, and they're all wrong.

"What I say is that it's the same wonderful, life-giving liquid, (only) the containers are different. That's what God is to me. And people are very caught up in the containers. So they mistake the container for the water – 'No, my container is right. It came direct from God;

I know it's true.' And it is true. But God speaks to us all. It's like a big wheel, and there's all kinds of ways to get to the center.

"Religion is a necessary component of human wholeness. When you look at religion from a historical point of view, you suddenly see that religion is a psychological aspect. We have to have religion. That is how we are. We have to relate to the fact that we're alive on this planet and we don't know how we got here. And we don't know why we're here, and we don't know where we're going.

"But there's good religion and bad religion. Good religion is what comes from within oneself, that makes one feel whole and good and in one piece, and joyful. Any time you find that, that's a great big bell in your head that you're doing the right thing. And it's different for different people."

One thing that all human beings most definitely have in common is death. And religious beliefs can provide the comfort in believing that life is eternal, that there is more to come after our time on Earth is through.

Mrs. Palmer says she, too, believes in an afterlife. She does not, however, presume to know what that might entail. One thing she is sure about is the existence of hell.

"That is such a ridiculous construct," she says. "I mean, think about it – it's childish. God is gonna send everybody and just cook 'em for eternity. I gave that one up a long time ago. I never heard Jesus talk about hell.

"All I know is that life is a very joyous thing, and when one opens up to the painfulness that life has, there is a tremendous richness. And there is no way that human life is an accident.

"I do think there is an after-life, and the reason I think that is because I have had an awful lot of experiences that tell me there is. But I don't know the ultimate, I really don't. We may explain all kinds of things, (and) how they happen, but we've only got part of the picture. And we really don't know what is at the bottom of it all, making it happen. But I have enough of an answer that I'm very content with my life as it is.

"My comfort is that God is with me all the time. I've had experiences that give me certainty that something of us goes on, past our physical existence. Where we go from there, I really don't know. It really doesn't matter. Even if, when I die, all of my molecules go back into the Earth and I'm recycled that way, that's OK with me.

Because I feel totally bonded to whatever my origin is. So, if I'm going to be a little chunk of dirt and a pebble and a snail and a blade of grass, that's OK, too. And I've never been able to say that before. I've always been terrified of dying. God isn't only good. He also taketh away – and he has to. You can't stay here forever."

In the meantime, Mrs. Palmer says she is excited about the future. A lifelong love of music and a chance meeting at the University of Houston downtown campus landed her a job singing with Robert Wilson's University of Houston Downtown Civic Jazz Orchestra. She also plans to continue her lifelong studies and enter a Houston seminary, where she hopes to earn a master's degree in pastoral counseling, before setting her sights on a career as a Jungian psychoanalyst. That could involve years of study, and maybe even a trip to Switzerland, the home of Carl Jung.

"God has always been there for me," she says. "And I really want to spend the rest of my life talking about God, and helping other people find who God is for them -- by finding out who they are."

§ § §

Chapter 22

"If God can take a person like me and turn me around, he can do it for anybody."

Chronic alcohol and drug abuse usually lead down a road that ends in one of two places: a cemetery or a jail cell. Shane Johnson of Marshall wound up in one of those spots, and figures he was headed for the other before God intervened.

Johnson, his wife and a friend were headed to his stepmother's house to mow the grass one evening in June 2002, when they stopped on the way to meet his sister-in-law in Kilgore. At that time, the self-described addict and alcoholic was in the midst of a two-year relapse after staying clean and sober for more than six years, following a 93-day stay in the county jail for check forgery.

"I had a cooler full of beer and three or four joints with me – my day was all planned, just the same as it had been for the past two years," Johnson remembers.

When they arrived, however, his wife's sister ran up to meet him, grabbed his hands and breathlessly said that she had a vivid dream with him in the starring role.

"She said, 'God has plans for you, (and) you need to change your life.' And I just had this overwhelming feeling that God had intervened. Just an overwhelming feeling that I'd had enough, and that God had plans for me. I haven't had a drink since."

Those plans apparently included the founding of Twelve-Way Foundation, a "continued recovery program" and halfway house for alcoholics and drug addicts near downtown Marshall, in far east Texas. Johnson started the non-profit outfit two years after that spiritual experience in Kilgore, when he met and befriended John Melton, a fellow recovering alcoholic from Fort Worth. They were introduced by a mutual friend.

"We just kind of tick-tocked around with the idea of a halfway house or three-quarter way house. Just the need for something like this in the community," Johnson, 31, explained. "Both of us have a strong belief that faith without works is dead. If you have made a decision, then the action should follow. So we started putting one foot in front of the other – letting God be the horse and us the carriage, and just following him. A house popped up, and then furniture popped up, and things just started rolling from there.

"We call it a sober living environment... with hopes that they'll become closer to God and be productive members of society."

Johnson, who was born in Tyler and started using drugs when he was 14 years old, says he "was taught good morals growing up," but had no formal religious training and was only an occasional churchgoer.

"I always considered myself an agnostic," he said. "I never was an atheist. I always believed there was a God, I just didn't know much about him."

After spending four months in a drug treatment center as a teenager, Johnson got high again three days after he was released and quickly found himself packed up by his mother and sent to live with his father in Atlanta, Ga. Within two weeks, he was in with a fast crowd, picking up where he left off with a drinking and drugging lifestyle that included a number of minor brushes with the law and an arrest for drunken driving. That behavior continued throughout high school and into the beginning of a college career that ended abruptly when his grandfather got seriously ill, and the young man moved back to Texas to care for him.

It was not long before he started forging checks from his grandfather's bank account to buy drugs, and he eventually got caught -- $5,065 worth. That landed him a three-month jail stay and Johnson stayed sober for "six years, two months and 15 days" after he got out, with the help of a 12-step recovery program.

During those six years, he got married and built a successful lawn service business with a crew of up to eight people working for him. Then, the business started going bankrupt and his father was diagnosed with terminal cancer. One day, he saw a half-smoked joint in the ashtray of an employee's truck. He picked it up and smoked it.

"I had a lot of issues going on, but the core issue was that I broke that conscious contact with God on a daily basis, and was turning back to my old ways of thinking – resentments, hatred, fear," Johnson says. "The only thing that stands between you and that drink or that drug is your relationship with God, and it wasn't there that day. And once I ingest those mind-altering substances into my system, it's just like a train going. It just don't stop.

"I thought, hell, won't nobody know. But I knew and God knew. And once I started, it was non-stop again for two years."

Along with his membership in a 12-step program for alcoholics, Johnson also belongs to a local Episcopal church. His Christian beliefs go hand-in-hand with the principles of the life-saving recovery program that also is a foundation for his halfway house.

"When I moved back to take care of my grandfather, he was going to a non-denominational church here in Marshall – that was in '93 – and I got saved before I sobered up. So I believe I turned my life over to Christ then, but turning my will over was a whole different thing.

"During the process of working the 12 steps, I developed a personal relationship with God, as I understand him. It's the same God of the Bible; Jesus Christ is my higher power. I pray every morning. I read scripture and my big book. God is everything to me today.

"I have feelings today that I call a God-consciousness, a sixth-sense of knowing right from wrong, good from bad, that I believe I've always had. But I believe God gave me free will, and I tend to misuse mine, so I turn it back over to him on a daily basis (through prayer). I just say, 'Let your will be done in my life.'

"I pray, and I wait for doors to open and I step in. If I'm not supposed to be there, they close real fast. The way it works for me is, I sometimes get persistent, constant thoughts about something, and I believe that can come from God – if it's in accordance with scripture. Like, if I have a constant thought all day to go rob a bank, I know that's not God speaking to me. But if it's to go help so-and-so, it probably is. If it's something along the line of what Christ teaches us, then it probably might be God's will. I believe that doors open and close, and it's my job to step through, not be afraid. Take a little baby step, and if it's God's will, I'll get a sign to take another little step.

"It's like being outside in the dark with a flashlight. You can only see as far as that light will take you; you can't see way on down the road.

"I don't know for sure what God's will is for me every day, but I know for sure what it's not, and that is to have fear, self-pity, hatred, dishonesty, guilt, shame. God forgives me, and loves and accepts me for who I am."

One area of their lives that both Johnson and Melton feel certain is in accordance with God's will is their halfway house. They are convinced that the facility is divinely inspired. A major reason for their assurance is a dream Melton had shortly after they founded the organization.

"In the beginning, this was funded by me and Shane," said Melton, a 50-year-old former construction worker who has been sober since March 14, 1999. "Everything just kind of came together, and we just said, 'Why not?' and started it. For awhile, it was pretty rough, because we were broke.

"There were doubts in the beginning. The first couple of months, we wondered whether this was going to work or not. Then I had a dream that I went to hell. And Jesus was standing right behind me -- I couldn't get my head turned around far enough to see him – and he had his hand on my shoulder, leading me around through a nightclub. And in this nightclub were people I had known throughout my life, who were not very morally stable people.

"I remember asking him, 'I'm trying to do so well; I turned my life around. Why am I here?' Then he took me outside, and we got in the car with somebody who had blood running down his face. We're driving down the road, and I'm worried because we're going fast and going up embankments and stuff, and this guy says, 'We can't die; we're already dead. We can have all the fun we want.'

"I thought, 'Oh, no, this is not what I wanted in life.' Then Jesus took me by the shoulder, and we started ascending, and I was happy because I thought I was on my way to heaven. But he put me back down, and when he put me back down, it was in a halfway house with the guys that we were working with. So I took that as a sign that this was where I needed to be.

"That's why I know God has his hand on our shoulders. It assured me that he was paying attention to what I was doing, and I knew I was doing the right thing."

A Fort Smith, Ark., native, Melton says he was raised as a Catholic, so he always believed in God, but never considered himself a faithful Christian. That lack of faith, however, does not explain the misfortunes he experienced throughout his drinking days.

"I don't think God punishes you," he says. "You're the one who causes your own problems. I'd go out and party on the weekend when my electric bill was overdue. What's going to happen when you do that? Your electric is going to get turned off. You can't blame God for that.

"I have always believed in God, known God. I went to Catholic school growing up, and if someone would ask me about God, I'd say, 'Yeah, I know God. I believe in God.' I just wasn't doing his will – didn't have that conscious contact. And if you're not doing his will, he don't have very good rewards for you.

"If God can take a person like me and turn me around, he can do it for anybody," said Melton, a divorced father and grandfather. "If you're doing the right thing, doors will open. If you're not doing the right things, doors will close on you. If you wake up in the morning and just ask God, 'Forgive me for my sins, and help me to learn your will, not mine,' you can sit there and think you made a bad decision, but somehow God will turn it into a good thing. But the harder you try and do it yourself, the worse it gets."

Johnson agrees. Life today for him is "peaceful, serene," despite a painful, degenerative back condition that has left him with several fused vertebrae and steel rods supporting his spine. Those physical problems prevent the father of two from working, but he says that, thus far, his rediscovered faith in God, daily prayer and good works are being rewarded. Financial hardships are a constant concern, but something always seems to happen to help him make ends meet.

"I thought, 'OK, I've got a family and I can't work no more. What's going to happen? We're going to lose everything.' But God has met my needs. Every need has been met. I still have the same house, same vehicles, got food on the table, satellite TV, everything," Johnson said.

"If we maintain that spiritual connection every day, and perform his work well – to me, that is loving others like he loves me – he provides my needs. It's all about that spiritual connection; trying to find God's will for us. I believe people weave in and out of our lives; some help us, and we help some.

"I don't know all the answers. What works for me, works. What works for other people may work for them. One thing I do know is this -- my understanding is not required. I leave it up to God."

§ § §

Chapter 23

"You can live in hell for eternity, or you can live in the streets of gold, and never have no pain and never be hungry. It's all up to you; it's that simple."

Del Rio native Bobbie Williams was a hard-living, truck-driving "thief and a thug" for most of his life before he decided to change his ways and become a Christian.

"I'd steal from you, lie to you, con you out of your money, (and) never go back and pay you. Buy something on credit, then go hide, go sell it, whatever. Whatever it took to make some money," Williams, 64, said. "For 51 years, that's the way I lived. I didn't know any better, because I wasn't taught. I don't have to do that any more, because God provides everything I need."

Now living in Abilene – a town of about 115,930 people located 200 miles west of Dallas -- with his wife, Susan, the retired trucker says he went to church throughout his childhood and always believed in God, but after a six-year stint in the U.S. Marine Corps in the 1960s, he started driving a truck for a living and drinking and chasing women for entertainment.

"I never was much on drugs, but I loved whiskey," Williams says. "I did all the things I thought a man was supposed to do: wine, women and song. Poppin' pills, running up and down the highway, going to beer joints, honky tonks, hookers... it didn't make any difference. Drank beer by the quarts. Rum, vodka, gin, whatever I could get. When it got to the point where I couldn't drink enough whiskey to get a buzz on, I quit.

"Had a pretty good time, but those days are over. Now, I have more fun being with my wife than anything else."

There was no lightning bolt from heaven, burning bush experience, or life-and-death crisis that turned him around, Williams says. Instead, it was a slow accumulation of misery that led him to seek help from what he believes is a power greater than himself.

"Let me ask you a question – what makes you eat?" Williams explains. "Hunger. When you're hungry, you want something to eat. You look for something to fill up that empty spot, whether it's pain, anger, love, whatever. It's all rolled into one ball of wax. You don't have to go through a big crisis, in order to be saved. The good Lord is there waiting on you. All you got to do is tell him you're ready. And when you accept him... all I can tell you is, if you don't want to go for it, you're the one who is going to have to pay the price, not me. I done paid my price.

"The price I paid? Fifty-one years of living like a dog. I wanted something better.

"Everybody has their problems, and if you don't have answers for those problems, you go somewhere to find it. I found mine through religion. My religion takes care of me. I worry about nothing – sickness, money, nothing.

"The only thing that (God) wants from you is your passion, desire and respect... to go to him. If you can't do that, you're lost. You're going to burn in hell. I know I ain't. And I'm not going to be setting there waiting on you with a towel – I'm going to be up there fanning myself, saying, 'Look at that damn fool down there.'

"I firmly believe that there's a stronger power than me going around just being a bum, running up and down the road."

Williams was baptized at age 51 at a church in Del Rio, a small southwest Texas city near the border with Mexico. At that time, he says he "felt the Holy Spirit coming into me," and a change began in his heart. His wife, Susan, who knew him for a long time before they were married, said the rough-and-tumble, illiterate trucker became a new man.

"He's not as hateful as he used to be," she said. "He's just very respectful, and very generous. If you need something and he has it, he'll give it to you."

Williams is a simple man, with simple beliefs. To go to heaven, he says, one must fully believe in the words and teachings contained in the Holy Bible. For him, there is one God and only one road to salvation and eternal life.

"The Bible says the majority of people will go to hell, because they don't believe in Jesus Christ," Williams says. "I put it this way... people can believe what they want to believe, and do what they want to do. But the way I believe in as a Christian, I'm not going to take a chance. Why should I? It's not worth it to me.

"You can live in hell for eternity, or you can live in the streets of gold, and never have no pain and never be hungry.

"There's a whole lot of people who ain't going (to heaven). And my mother-in-law is one of 'em. She don't believe in Jesus as the Messiah. She believes in the Jewish religion... and I don't know nothing about it, so I don't know what she believes in.

"Look, it's whatever you want. Do you want to burn for eternity, or do you want to live? Simple as that. That's my opinion. The preacher one day said, 'I can see my name up there in the letters, in red. Up there by Jesus, at the left hand of God.' I said, 'Yeah, OK. I couldn't see mine there.' He said, 'Why?' I said, 'I see mine in gold.'

"I don't contribute it to being a better Christian. It's just something I feel. If you want something bad enough, you're going to get it, I don't care who it is. If you go to the good Lord and talk to him (about your problems), he will answer you. And in his time, he will provide. It's just like anything else."

Williams spends a lot of his time now traveling around the state with his wife and their two Chihuahua dogs. Life is good, he says, and it doesn't take much to make him happy.

"There's some regrets, but not many," William said. "And it don't amount to a hill of beans. Everybody has regrets.

"Life is what you make of it. I'm enjoying my life now. I sit down and have my supper, and I feel blessed. Because if it wasn't for him, I wouldn't have it. A lot of people don't feel that way, but I do. Before I become a Christian, I had nothing. And after I become a Christian, I got everything -- a lovely wife, a home that's paid for, three trucks that's paid for, six trailers that's paid for. I live pretty good. I'm not in too bad of health... 50 percent of my kidneys are gone and I'm a diabetic, but I don't worry about it. Because I got somebody else doing the worrying for me.

"A color TV with a remote control, a full belly and a full glass of iced tea – that's all I want. That's all I ever wanted."

§ § §

Chapter 24

"The emptiness that I felt on the inside, I wanted to be felt somewhere on the outside. And the only way I knew to try and do that was possibly through suicide."

Chris Sammons was 17 years old when the heartache of broken dreams and disappointment grew too much to bear and he found himself wanting to die. As he prepared to carry out a plan to end his suffering, a message of love and hope he says was divinely inspired came over his car radio.

"The plan that I had in my head was to take my Ford Mustang, which I loved very much, and drive around the loop in Nacogdoches as fast as I could and see how many flips I could take in the car," Sammons says. "Because not only would I take my life, but I also would take the last thing that I cared about on this Earth – which was my car – with me.

"The emptiness that I felt on the inside, I wanted to be felt somewhere on the outside. And the only way I knew to try and do that was possibly through suicide. That's how low I had gone. The emptiness and pain that was on the inside... I knew at that moment, it would be felt on the outside.

"I remember sitting in my car early one morning, ready to do it," he said. "I turned on the car, and for some reason there was a Christian station playing on the radio. It reminded me of God's love for me, and it reminded me of the way I felt about God way back when I was seven years old and first accepted the Lord. I think it was God's way of saying, 'I'm still here.' Because of that... I believe it was only because of God's grace that I did not take my life that day. It literally saved my life."

Sammons recounted that emotional story during a break in his duties as minister of students for the Baptist Student Ministry at his alma mater, Stephen F. Austin State University in Nacogdoches. The West Palm Beach, Fla., native earned a bachelor's degree in speech communications there, before completing his master's degree in divinity at Southwestern Seminary in Fort Worth.

Armed with those credentials, and considering his occupation, it is fairly easy to identify Sammons as a man of faith and strong convictions. That was not always the case, however.

The 31-year-old father of two boys said he "grew up going to church" with his parents, and came to believe in God and the principles of Christianity at the tender age of seven.

"I knew that I was a sinner and that there was a separation between me and God, and that Jesus Christ was the way to help reconcile that relationship with God -- obviously, I didn't understand all that as a seven-year-old, but what I could understand was that I was a sinner and that Jesus died for me," he explained. "I accepted that, and continued to live and learn what that meant."

Life was good and the family eventually moved to Nacogdoches, a bustling and historic city of around 30,000 people in the heart of East Texas that began as a Caddo Indian settlement, and is known as the oldest town in the state.

Then, as he entered his teen years, the young boy's world turned upside down when his parents announced they were getting a divorce. He was in junior high school, and everything he had learned about life and about God suddenly did not make sense.

"Everything that I had come to understand, I automatically began to question," he recalls. "Because that didn't seem to be the type things that the God I came to understand... those were not the qualities that I began to feel and understand, so I began to question some of that. So there was a period of my life that I went through quite a bit of rebellion – from my parents, but also from God."

That rebellion became more and more pronounced as Sammons entered high school and got more heavily involved in drinking, a hard-partying lifestyle and unhealthy relationships. He was trying to soothe that damaged part of his soul with any type of remedy he could find, until he ran out of answers and found himself behind the wheel of his car, contemplating the possible end of his life.

"It was pretty serious," Sammons said. "I tried everything the world says is going to give you happiness. Anything that I thought would bring satisfaction, I tried at some point in time, ultimately to find that it did not bring satisfaction -- or if it did, it was only momentary satisfaction, and ultimately led to a greater emptiness in my life, and I began to feel a void that I had not experienced before.

"I had broken up with my girlfriend, and had gone to a party where I drank so much that I began to dry-heave (vomiting); there was nothing left in my stomach. It was just miserable. The people I had grown to love so much (his parents), on some level had let me down with (the end of) their relationship. Now my girlfriend had let me down. The relationships I had with friends, which were mostly based on alcohol, had let me down. So I had nowhere else to turn."

Then, the message from that Christian radio station on his car stereo reminded him of the day 10 years earlier, when an innocent little boy decided to put his faith and trust in a God he hardly understood. It was the turning point in his life.

"The best that I knew how, I rededicated my life to the Lord right there in the car, and just said, 'God, I don't understand what all's gone on, but as best as I know how, I give you whatever is left of this life.' And I went to church that next Sunday," Sammons said. "I knew from that point that God was at work.

"I just began to take steps that I had grown up being taught to take, but never really took because I felt it had been forced on me. All of a sudden, it became necessary for my survival. I guess I just began to do the things that I knew all along I was supposed to do, and it became something that was helping me, that I very much felt was God's presence guiding me. I got my life straightened out, and realized that I wasn't living for people any more, inasmuch as I was living for the Lord.

"It was kind of a slow process. A lot of folks that were my friends – some of those relationships changed quite a bit because of my new way of living, my new lifestyle. I had a lot of friends who were skeptical about the changes going on in my life. A lot folks would say things like, 'Oh, this will only last six months, and then he'll be back to the way he was.' So it was a tough thing, especially going into your senior year in high school. A lot of things changed, but there was a satisfaction in my life that didn't require the approval of those friends. And as my relationship with God grew over the next couple of years, I began to understand what it meant to live for the Lord.

"There was a youth minister at our church who left, and when he left, there was an opportunity for me to go and lead some Bible study and stuff, and through leading those things, I kind of felt like that was something God would allow me to do for the rest of my life. Through those circumstances and situations, I began to feel led to the ministry... a lot of the things I had gone through, there were a lot of people I knew that were going through some of the same kind of things, and so being able to share that story with other people, knowing that they were in similar situations, to share with them the hope that I had found in Christ is the reason why I got into ministry."

Although he is obviously well-versed in the Bible and religious history, and has a rock-solid faith, Sammons admits that he does not have all the answers to life's most perplexing questions. In fact, after all these years he sometimes faces the same struggles as some of the visitors to his office. Why do bad things happen to good people? Why does a loving God allow people to suffer unbearable agony? Why does God send people to hell? Why are we here?

In the end, he said, understanding the mysteries of life and the puzzle of God often comes down to a simple matter of faith and acceptance.

"Christianity is a messy thing," Sammons says. "Our spiritual life is a messy thing. We are on a journey, and as we go on this journey, a lot of things that come up, there are no easy answers for. There are certainly times, even since I have started in ministry, when I have wondered, 'Where is God?'

"And I think we miss the boat sometimes when we fail to struggle with God, and we fail to ask God the hard questions, because we are afraid of the answers he'll give us. Sometimes, maybe it is that we ask the questions, but we really don't want to know the answer. And in fact, I think that sometimes when we struggle through the questions, that is when the real answers are found. But all too often, we give it the easy answers.

"In the midst of this crisis, or that crisis, we wonder, 'Why does he at times seem to play hide-and-seek with us?' There is a Christian author who has written that if God does play hide-and-seek with us, it's not so much because he loves to hide, it's because he loves to be found. And I think there's a lot of truth to that. Maybe sometimes things happen in our lives because God does want us to struggle through things, and come closer to understanding who he is. I certainly think that is part of the process.

"But Christianity is ultimately about faith. It's the substance of things hoped for and not seen," he said. "Sometimes it's a blind faith, but it doesn't have to be an uneducated faith. We don't have to throw our minds and senses out the window when we accept Christ. I don't think we have to throw away all of the questions we have, just because we've accepted Christ."

As a Christian, Sammons believes that the only way he can reach heaven is by accepting in his heart that Jesus Christ is his personal savior, the son of God who was sent from heaven to die on the cross to atone for the sins of all mankind. He stops short of condemning other religions, and says that whatever path a man takes in the search to learn more about God, if he looks long and hard enough, he will eventually find the right answer.

"I do believe in what the Bible teaches. Jesus himself said, 'I am the way, the truth and the life. No man comes to the father except by me.' Those are Jesus' own words; they're not my words. And I don't know of any way of getting around that. I don't think that if you pray to Buddha, you will spend eternity in heaven, simply because Buddha is not the way to heaven.

"I would say that Jesus is the only way, but I would also suggest that when we are seeking God, that he has a way of revealing himself to you, and ultimately I think that will lead you to a relationship with Jesus Christ," Sammons said.

"For a lot of people, the generic idea of God is not a big problem. It gets to be more of an issue when you bring up the name, Jesus Christ. When that happens, what was once OK to talk about is all of a sudden no longer OK to talk about. And I think part of that is simply because when you speak of Jesus Christ, you have to do something with him. When you're confronted with the person of Jesus Christ, you either have to accept him or reject him. There's no in-between. And automatically, that can become a confrontational issue. I think that's probably part of the main reason.

"People say, 'What about the African in the deep bush that has never heard?' I think that in God's grace there are opportunities for those folks. Again, I think part of the problem with who we are is that we think Christianity is a nice, neat box. The truth of the matter is that Christianity is not nice and neat; it's a messy thing. There is no easy answer. And because of that, I think we must interact with a God that is personal, that reveals himself to us and is ours. To say, 'Ah-hah, I'm going to stay away from that group of people or this group of people,' I don't think that is part of God's nature.

"The scripture teaches us that God desires that all men be saved, but God doesn't force himself on any of us. There's no way that he can. I don't think he's going to force us to love him, or do anything. So I think the choice of whether we accept him or not is just that – it's our choice. And because it is our choice, I don't know that we can necessarily say that God is the one who sends us to hell. It is a choice that we make. I know that's not an easy answer, and it's not a complete answer.

"Does God punish people? I think that just as any loving father disciplines his children, yeah, I think there is some element of discipline that takes place. If you think about the Old Testament and how the people of Israel turned away from God, and how there were consequences for that... I think that is still true today. If you turn away and do things that are against God, there are certain consequences that are part of that.

"I see no other answer, except a relationship with Jesus Christ. If you accept what the Bible says to be true, if the Bible is true – and I believe that it is – then there is no other way."

While the world at times seems a chaotic place devoid of the spirit of a loving and caring creator, Sammons says his experience clearly demonstrates the personal connection that is available between man and God. He believes his life was spared for a reason, and that reason is to help others find what he has found.

"I think God is intimately involved in our lives – or as much as we allow him to be. I don't think God is a watchmaker that just makes the watch and then allows it to keep ticking, without ever having to do anything. I don't believe he has just made his creation, and is allowing things to tick. Even in my own life, I think if I had not turned on my Mustang and heard that Christian radio station that reminded me of his faithfulness in the past... I think that was his personal activity in my life.

"The God that is very personal to me cares about what is going on in my life, and in my family's life, but he's also at work in the world, in other's lives.

"I think ultimately, our purpose in life is to bring glory to God, in whatever that may be. That could be whether you are a newspaper reporter, a school teacher, a minister or a mechanic. I think there is a purpose in life when we do those things to bring honor and glory to God. Were we created to worship (God)? Yeah, absolutely. I think scripture teaches us that we are, by nature, worshippers. And I think our ultimate purpose in life is found in that. But I think it is also found as we bring glory to the Lord. Whatever you do, the scripture says do it all to the glory of God."

§ § §

Chapter 25

"I think life is a school. We're here to grow and to learn, but mainly to love. Love is the power; God is love."

Every religion throughout the world contains the ultimate truth, according to the Rev. John Benson of Amarillo. Unfortunately, he says, most of those faiths also include a number of fallacies that too often stand in the way of spiritual development and growth.

"I can go to the Baptist or the Lutheran or any other church, sit down and glean the truth that is presented," Benson said. "When you love God and you love your fellow man, after that -- whatever philosophy fills your needs is right for you.

"Now, if you are happy in that philosophy where there is a belief in duality, a heaven and a hell, a good and an evil… there is only one power, not two. What we call 'evil' is a misuse of the one power. It is giving power to the negative, which doesn't exist. God is all there is, and there isn't anything else. There can't be two infinites. One infinite.

"Satan is a recognition of something that really does not exist, but since people believe in it and since they accept it as a power, then for them, it acts as though it were. But it's like being afraid of going into a dark basement. The darkness is not a power – it's the absence of light. And when you bring the light in, what happens to the darkness? It disappears. So there is no devil; there is no hell. There is just an absence of light. It is a belief in duality that is holding man back. It is a belief in separation from God.

"There is no separation. God is within us all. God is the absolute spirit and essence of all that we know life to be. It is the creative power in the universe; it is the substance of which we all are made; it is the source and foundation of all that we see. It is a life force, expressing itself in many ways. At the human level, we believe it is the highest expression of that intelligence, as it individualizes itself in man and woman. The life that is within me is the supreme intelligence expressing itself, through you and through me. We're all one. God is the life of each one of us – it's God's life that we are all living -- and as we listen and are open and receptive to its promptings, or its intuition, we discover the nature of this infinite life and love and principle of being. God is all there is."

Benson, a 61-year-old Chicago native, is the newly appointed leader of the Unity Church congregation in Amarillo, a city of 170,000-plus in the far north Texas panhandle. He was raised a Catholic, but began to look elsewhere for his spiritual education and nourishment after coming to the realization that, according to his religion upbringing, he appeared to be heading for eternal damnation.

"At some point, I realized that if the Catholics – and the Protestants -- were right in their presentation, I would probably wind up going to the 'hot place,' Benson explained. "Just living at the human level, thinking there was only one life to live, and that at the time – when you die – you would be judged based on what went on here. But that's not in line with the true teachings of the ages. See, we're not looking at a certain philosophy as being the only way. There are many paths. Many roads lead to the father's house. Because of a lack of understanding, I accepted what I was taught. But then there was a desire to change, to know the truth and expand my awareness of why I'm here and what is my purpose for being.

"So through further study, and especially when I met my wife – who already had this higher awareness – then I began to search, and I realized that man is a spiritual being. And that regardless of appearances to the contrary, he is made in the perfect image and likeness of God, and his consciousness and his awareness will expand and unfold in the right way and at the right time. And his efforts to cooperate and to know the truth will probably bring that event much sooner... where he has reached that point in consciousness where there's the awareness of this Christ self. It might be called the Buddha consciousness in another presentation of the truth.

"I think life is a school. We're here to grow and to learn, but mainly to love. Love is the power; God is love. And the consciousness of love is the highest consciousness in the universe. To the degree that we're able to let that love express itself through us, to that degree are we healed. And to that degree are we powerful.

"I believe we're all here because a higher intelligence put us here. I think every individual is here because their consciousness is a part of the divine ideal for whatever that higher intelligence is trying to express, by means of the life on this planet. Our purpose is to discover and awaken to who we are. If we all lived in the aborigine state, eventually someone would know, 'There's got to be more than this.' All progress is based on a desire to go beyond the levels that the human race has achieved. And that's great, but it's a combination of the spiritual, the mental and the physical that completes the trinity, if you will.

"So, the purpose for each person being here would be to awaken to the truth of their being, and contribute creatively to life and its expression by means of their talents and abilities, to try and leave the world a better place than they found it. And to contact the spirit and engage in communion with it, for the purpose of receiving the influx of its wisdom and light. I don't know any other way to live at that higher level. And that in no way puts down any other lifestyles or anything like that.

"You have to continue to grow in consciousness. You can't stop and say, 'OK, I have arrived.' It's an eternal quest. That's what some mystics have called it – 'the eternal quest for self-realization.' And then to live and to act from that high state of awareness."

Benson's philosophy of 'practical Christianity' is centered around four principles: affirmative prayer, spiritual healing, the teachings of Jesus and learning about the workings of the conscious and subconscious mind. While his beliefs do not coincide with traditional Christian interpretations of the Bible, he says the words of Jesus provide a model for the way a person's life should be lived.

"Jesus remains the great way-show-er. He remains the elder brother for all of us," Benson said. "I'm sure that the crucifixion experience was the result of being politically incorrect. Certainly, it was not something that the infinite intelligence would require of anyone... but, also, if that was the fulfilling of a prophecy, I can see where someone of that high consciousness would be willing to do that, (and) if along the way, it would help people to find a contact to make them feel that, yes, no matter what had happened, someone took their place and sacrificed their life in a way that would affect the greater good of the planet.

"Jesus came at a time when he was needed. So his consciousness still affects everyone on the planet who is open to it. And then, he was able to resurrect (his) human temple – a person of higher power can do that, I believe, absolutely. Even though they would normally appear to be dead, they could resurrect or in some way manifest a similar vehicle, which would allow people to recognize them. I think people cross over and then come back and appear. People have seen apparitions – what they call ghosts – and they've seen manifestations. I just believe in all possibilities, so it really has nothing to do with any particular church presentation.

"It may be that he was able to survive the entire incident. Once they got permission to take down the body, he may have not given up the ghost, but was able to make that appearance. But whether it is or it isn't (true) doesn't really make any difference. It's where we are today in consciousness, in our desire to realize the true self, the God within.

"We know that this God, with its infinite mind, is waiting to be called upon. There is no separation (between man and God). There is only right here, and right now. As (the apostle) Paul said, 'Awaken, though that sleepest, and Christ shall give thee life.' It's like having a million dollars in the bank, and not knowing it. Doesn't do you a lot of good. But all of a sudden, someone says someone has left you an estate of a million dollars. Well, you just move right into that.

"Life is ever new. And every individual, no matter what they've done or how many lives they've lived, makes it back to the father's house. God is love, and God is law. It's all a big cosmic dream and drama, and we're all players in it. As Shakespeare said, 'In his life, man plays many roles.' But in the end, God is playing all the roles. There's one life, and it's God – that's it. You say, 'Why would God do this; why would God do that?' Every individual has freedom of choice; freedom to express their divinity in positive and/or negative ways. In other words, there's a spiritual power, and you can use it affirmatively or negatively. But the way the principle works is, as a man thinketh in his heart, so is he. Whatsoever you give it, you get back. Whatever every man soweth, that shall he also reap.

"We live in a spiritual universe of laws and principles. If I stick my hand in the electrical socket, I'm going to get shocked. But, I understand the principle. So if I connect the wires right, I can use electricity until kingdom come, so to speak.

"Ralph Waldo Emerson calls God 'the oversoul.' So, the supreme intelligence that governs the universe will also govern and direct our affairs, if we allow it to do so -- if we expect it; if we believe it; if we work in such a manner that we make ourselves instruments and channels through which this divine wisdom and love can express. So as Jesus said, 'Of mine own self, I can do nothing. It is the father in me that does the work.' That's the way I look at it. At the human level, I can only do so much. But there's a higher power and intelligence that governs the universe, and will govern my affairs if I believe it, accept it and give thanks for it. The universe is perfect, and man is awakening to that perfection."

Prayer, meanwhile, is a powerful force for change and spiritual growth and improvement, Benson says, and he believes that God does indeed hear and answer prayers. Again, however, not in the traditional sense. For prayer to be effective, one's entreaties must be affirmations of one's wishes and desires. In other words, believe that your prayers have been answered, and they are.

"God answers prayer through a scientific principle, which does unto each as they believe. Appearances would certainly indicate that there are miracles. But, in the end, God always answers prayer. I think that would be a maxim: 'God always answers prayer.' Now, whatever sorts of things you desire when you pray, believe that you have received them and you shall. So successful prayer is based on a mental equivalent, or a realization, that the idea that you are seeking to demonstrate in your life has already been expressed and demonstrated.

"In prayer, what we are simply seeking to do is take the idea at the conscious level, impress it on the subconscious, and then having impressed it and felt it to be true, the subconscious mind – which is the individual's access to infinite intelligence and power – accepts that and begins to give it form. That creates a thought form, which the universal substance by which all things are made fills. Everything begins with a thought, and the infinite intelligence and the subconscious work together to bring that thought into form.

"So, to learn how to think is to learn how to live. Repetition, faith and expectancy. When you pray, you pray from the standpoint that your good is already at hand. It is already complete, in the mind of God. Prayer is a series of mental movements which lead you from the point of 'I need it,' to 'I have it.' It is praying with the knowing that there is a divine intelligence which receives the direct impress of our thought, and acts upon it creatively. We're praying all day long – our thoughts are our prayers.

"Man is what he thinks about all day long. So, when you pray, believe you received it, and you get it. It may not come in the form that you expect it, but... whatever you are praying for, it is that or something better. In the end, it's a realization of the presence of God that is the most healing agency in the universe. The higher intelligence that is at work in the universe that can only give you (things) at your ability to accept.

"Whatever you pray for, take the idea that you have received it, accept it, give thanks as if you've already received it. Do your part: make the phone calls, look at the want ads, follow through with your quest that will lead you to the steps where you want to go.

"Whatever it is, if you have that desire, the infinite wants to give it to you. You just have to establish in your mind the consciousness of it. Everything is consciousness – 'To him that hath, it shall be given. To him that hath not, it shall be taken away; even that which he has.' That is the principle. Why? Because to him that hath not, that person has a consciousness of lack and limitation. Therefore, that produces more lack. The consciousness of 'all the father hath is mine; all power is given unto me,' as a spiritual being.

"Life is to be lived from the inside out – it's a spiritual trip. In my profession – ministry – my business is to keep expanding my consciousness and to help others find spiritual healing."

Heaven and hell, meanwhile, and life after death, are concepts for which Benson has philosophies that stray somewhat from the mainstream viewpoint.

"I do not believe in heaven and hell as actual places, but as states of consciousness within each one of us. Jesus said, 'The kingdom of heaven is within you.' So heaven can certainly be described as that state of awareness in which there is perfect peace, and in which we realize our unity of being with the creator. I would think that heaven would be that realm of perfect peace within each one of us. Because there is no other life – God indwells all people.

"Death is a term given by medical science when cessation of life energy in this body temple occurs. But I really believe in my heart that there is no death. When we leave the body temple, and the silver cord is broken, that spiritual energy and life that we are moves to that plane of consciousness which reflects where we are in the (spiritual development) of our soul. I think there are different planes of life – 'In my father's house, there are many mansions.'

"I believe that life is eternal, and I believe that we are here going through various experiences and circumstances, and eventually we reach that place where we're back with the infinite, to whatever degree that would be," he said. "I don't believe in an eternity where you're stuck in one place with harps and angels, but since this infinite mind and intelligence of God is constantly creating, then creation is never-ending."

As for ways to achieve maximum spiritual growth and become closer to God, to achieve peace of mind, contentment and true happiness, Benson says the answer all returns to love. Loving God, and loving people. Education and study lead to understanding, he says, and understanding leads to wisdom. That in turn leads to the ability to get in touch with the spiritual power that he believes resides within us all.

"Love is the best work -- that is why we're here," the 61-year-old father of four says. "The most important thing an individual must learn to do really is to understand the nature of mind and consciousness. When you understand the nature of mind and consciousness, then you open your mind up to the higher wisdom and intelligence of the spirit. God is desiring to share its love and its wisdom and its power with its creation.

"It happens in different ways to different people. But I think it's a desire to know the truth. Jesus said, 'And ye shall know the truth, and the truth shall make you free.' The truth is the same today, yesterday and forever.

"Meditation is opening the mind to God. It's a very powerful avenue of inspiration, illumination and enlightenment. That's what we're all seeking. The whole trip is love, and it's enlightenment, illumination, inspiration. So, it's prayer, meditation, study, communion with spirit.

"Even men and women who live the worst life, so to speak... Paul, who is given credit for the beginnings of Christianity, was a murderer. Moses was a murderer. We don't care. We aren't interested in Jesus being crucified; we aren't interested in his death. We are interested in his life; his teachings. To follow his teachings, and to know that the Christ consciousness which animated and expressed its perfection through him is (also) within us, and does the same through those who choose to allow it to do so.

"It's a never-ending search for a higher, greater good, which is within. Spiritual man is perfect, whole and complete, (and) the individualized expression – incapable of being divided – of the infinite mind and spirit of God. So we look upon these great leaders, and each one adds something to the puzzle, the mysteries of life. You can't know it all, because you can't comprehend the infinite with a finite mind. And even when you get to the point where you think you can, infinity keeps on going. There is no end. Wherever we are, God is. So in the twinkling of an eye, things could change, and we could be in the depths of hell. And the next moment, due to a change in consciousness on our part, good happens and the negative lesson is over.

"As James Allen says in 'As A Man Thinketh,' he said when man radically alters his thinking, he will be amazed at the rapid transformation that takes place in the conditions and circumstances of his life.

"God indwells all men and women. There are no sinners; there are no saints. Just some people have risen to a higher level of awareness. I'm not saying some people don't deserve the title of sainthood, but that's not what they're interested in, in the first place. It's not about religion; it's about spirituality. That's the whole thing. Our goal is to recognize the Christ in all people, and to do everything we can to help them realize it.

"Speak to the God within you. Be thankful. The heart full of gratitude receives multiplied blessings. We live in a universe of spiritual principles, and when you understand the nature of the principle and use it, you get the result you desire. To him who loves much, much is forgiven. You have to forgive; you have to love; you have to give; you have to make it your business to find the indwelling of God, whatever pathway that takes.

"The Buddha said, 'The mind is everything.' Whatever you think, you become. Good thoughts produce good circumstances."

§ § §

Chapter 26

"God is the pure essence of love..."

Forget about heaven and hell, repentance and redemption, good and evil and most other traditional religious teachings. According to Bill Douglas, a Fort Worth hypnotherapist and spiritual counselor, everyone will eventually reach an eternal paradise, though it may take several cycles of reincarnation to reach a lofty enough psychic plane to get there.

"God is the essence of pure love, and God cannot conceive of you ever doing anything wrong – he only sees you as being perfect," Douglas says. "And there actually is no right or wrong; there never has been. There are consequences for what you do, but there is no right and wrong. It just is.

"The real God would never give you a set of ten commandments saying, 'Thou shalt not...' He would never do that, because you have free will. Why would he take that away from you? Yes, you have a free will, except for these ten things? That's baloney. There are really only two commandments: to love the Lord God with all thy soul, all thy heart and all thy strength; and to love your fellow man the same way God loves you. Other than that, you are responsible for anything and everything that happens to you.

"Everything about your life is set up ahead of time," he explains. "Before you are born, you sit down with your primary guide and a guardian angel that is assigned to you, according to where you are on your spiritual path. They are perfectly matched to you, and you can't incarnate (inhabit a human body) without those two entities. It is impossible. You sit down with them and write out your script, your play. Then you have to go out and get people to interact in your play. You're not a one-man show. You and I have known one another before. You don't run into anybody that you have not set it up ahead of time to run into. And they're there for a reason. It may seem just like a passing thing, but they're there for a reason.

"When you are born, your personality is determined by your name. And you give your parents your name. They don't name you; you name you. You put it in their head, whatever it is you want to be named. Then you decide which day you want to be born on, because that sets up your destiny.

"Because of that, everybody is totally responsible for what happens to them – whether they get abused, whether they are murdered, whether they go over to Iraq and get their arm blown off... hey, you wrote the script. What are you complaining about? The sooner you realize that, the quicker you're going to move along."

Unlike conventional religious doctrine, the belief system Douglas follows – he refers to it simply as 'Spirituality' – centers around a somewhat complex heavenly hierarchy that basically includes a supreme God at the top, followed by "the only begotten son," then an eternal paradise with a paradise father and paradise sons. In a cosmic nutshell, the ultimate goal for human beings is to mature enough spiritually through a series of reincarnations to become a paradise son, which is a master who rules over a cosmic day. A cosmic day encompasses a number of universes, and there are "untold numbers" of cosmic days throughout all of creation.

"About 15 billions years ago, this universe was created," Douglas, 63, explains, relaxing in his downtown area living room. "And it was the first time that anybody had ever gone into materiality. Before that, we were always just free spirits moving around... and whenever we wanted something, the materialization would occur at the same time the thought was occurring. And when the thought was complete, whatever it was that you wanted was complete at the same time.

"We didn't even understand how to do that; we could just do it. It was instant – and it was boring. Because you could do anything you wanted to do.

"So an experiment was set up for us to come in and experience being masters of limitation. Before that, we were totally unlimited. So we came in under an entity that called itself Yahweh, who is the God of the Old Testament -- and he's not the supreme God. He made you believe he was God when he came in, but he was a local Jewish god and that was all he was. God is the essence of pure love, and in the Old Testament it shows God as leading the Jews into battle, and punishing people, doing this and doing that. A God that is pure love would never do something like that.

"And so you've been kicking around in this universe – I call it the arena – for about 15 billion years. The whole idea here was to throw the dark forces and the light forces into an arena and see how it worked out. To see if they could come together and work things out peaceably. The lights forces think they're the good guys, and the dark forces think they're the good guys. So they look down on each other, they don't get along, and the bottom line is, it's just not going to happen. The experiment has failed.

"And the thing about it is, the thing we're in here is called the Grand Illusion. This is not real. All of this is an illusion. Everything on this planet is a holographic image, including you and including me. This lamp, this couch, this house, your car – everything is a holographic image. It's not real.

"Everybody is looking for a way home (to heaven), but there is nothing to seek," he says. "You are where you already want to be. You're already home. All you have to do is stop and realize, 'Hey, I'm already there; all I have to do is wake up.' And most of the time your (spiritual) guides and your angels are telling you, 'Wake up.' That's their message to you. Because none of this is real. And when you wake up, you come into the peace that passes all understanding that Jesus talks about in the Bible.

"Everybody is going home, sooner or later," Douglas said. "How long it takes you to get there is up to you. How many times you get diverted off your path is under your control. If you allow the dark forces to divert you off the path, that's OK. God doesn't have any feelings about it one way or the other. He is patient. And the farther along you go on the path, the more you wake up and the higher you move up in the hierarchal chain." Douglas, who was born in Oklahoma City and grew up as a self-proclaimed Air Force brat, has been a certified hypnotherapist for 14 years, and first began experimenting with hypnosis when he was 17 years old. He has studied and practiced numerology, a system of using numbers to determine a person's destiny and life path, and attended Tarrant County College, Texas Christian University and The Atwood Institute in Arizona.

The divorced father of a son and daughter was a longtime Episcopalian, an usher and a Sunday school teacher, until he severed all ties with the church in the late 1980s during what he calls "a dark time" in his life.

"I had been a member of that church for years," he said. "My grandmother had been a member, my mother, my brothers... and I was really down one day, and I wanted to talk to a priest. I went over there and I said, 'I'd like to talk to a priest.' And the lady said, 'Are you a member of this church?' I said, 'I used to be.' And she said, 'Oh, you have to be a member or they won't talk to you.'

"Where do they get off saying that kind of shit? I didn't need them.

"I had just gotten divorced, and my wife had turned my kids totally against me – I couldn't even see them. I was at a really down point. I remember sitting in this little house I was living in, thinking, 'Do I really want to go on with this any more?' And I looked up in the corner of the ceiling and I saw the angel of death looking at me. He said, 'Well?' I said, 'You need to leave.' Then a voice came to me that said, 'I'm going to take you on a journey. Are you ready to do it?'
"

It was that voice that led him to embark on 20 years of exploration and study, trying to find peace of mind and answers to mankind's eternal questions. Two books have been key in his discoveries: "The Keys of Enoch," and "The Urantia Book." And he now considers himself firmly grounded in a faith that he admits is decidedly unorthodox, but one that contains what he believes to be the truth.

"You have to have an open mind, and most people on this planet don't have an open mind," he said. "God is the center and the all of everything. You are God; I am God – otherwise we wouldn't exist, because God is everything. There is absolutely nobody in all of creation, not one single entity, that is holier than you. Not Jesus. Not Buddha. Not Mohammed. Not anybody. There is nobody more holy than me. There is nobody less holy than either one of us.

"Most people operate out of fear-based emotions. I don't have any fear-based emotions, because I don't buy into the illusion. How can you fear something that is not real?

"I ask a lot of people, 'Are you satisfied with where you are?' If you're not satisfied with where you are, maybe the ego doesn't need to run the show any more. Maybe God does. I never know where anything's coming from. If I try to interject a time frame or a limit or a map or anything like that, I'm getting in the way. And God steps back and says, 'OK, whenever you decide to get out of the way, I'll take back over again.'

"That's the surrender. You surrender your ego back to God."

Douglas says his spiritual condition is such that he is able to walk around in a near-constant state of meditation, always ready to take direction and receive insights from God. He does not believe in the power of prayer, which he says is a self-defeating exercise. Instead, he opts for a form of mantra, or chanting, similar to the Hindu method of worship and reflection.

"You really think you need to pray? Now, since your mind is inextricably linked to God, and your thoughts are really not your own and they are God's anyway, don't you think he knows what you need before you are even aware of it? So, why would you need to pray for it?

"Everything in the universe is in reverse," Douglas says. "The universe looks down at you, and the universe loves you unconditionally and they'll do anything they can for you. Whatever you focus on is what you're going to get more of. If you're praying for money to meet the rent, buy groceries, make the car payment, how do you think the universe sees that?

"The universe looks at it and sees that you are focused on lack. And they're saying, 'Oh, he wants more lack. We'll give him more.' This is what is meant by everything is in reverse.

"The church works with what they call faith. That is their key word. And that key word implies that you don't have it. If you go around saying, 'I have faith,' all you're saying to the universe is, 'I don't.' Guess what you're going to get?

"Instead of praying, if you will say and live the following two things, your life will change dramatically, and it will happen very quickly. Those two things are: 'God is the sole source of all my supply; I always have more than I need before I know I need it.'

"The final thing, which is the hardest step for anybody to do on this planet, is to surrender. Because your ego is going to fight you tooth and nail. But if you're saying God is the sole source of your supply and you always have more than you need before you need it, ego is not involved in that at all.

"He wants to know that you understand that it's coming from him. And when you acknowledge that, you get even more."

§ § §

Chapter 27

"God is... "

So... what do I think about God? Hell, I don't know – oops, no pun intended. About all I can say for sure is that I do believe in God. Absolutely. Thanks to an unforgettable spiritual experience I had in May 1989, in which a true miracle of some sort saved my life, I can never honestly doubt the existence of some sort of God, or higher power.

Now, having said that, I don't know who God is, what he looks like, where he lives, or why he does the things he does. And when I say 'he,' who knows? God may be female. Or male and female. Or neither male nor female. A good friend of mine in Austin refers to God as she. Some people refer to God as 'it,' a genderless, omnipresent, universal life force that lives inside us all.

God is like the ocean, some say, and we humans are like droplets of ocean water. Parts of the whole. And when we die, we return to our source, like droplets of ocean water returning to the sea.

Nevertheless, assuming for the sake of argument that God is a supreme being who created the Earth, the stars, the sun, the moon and everything else – including human life -- according to some sort of mystical, supernatural plan that culminates with heavenly salvation and/or eternal damnation, I have to say that God is a little strange.

OK, let me clarify that statement. God is not strange. God is mysterious. Hard to understand. But some of the things that are attributed to God are very strange indeed.

As my wife and I returned home one Saturday evening from seeing the Mel Gibson movie, "Passion of Christ," at a theater in Killeen, the largest city in our little neck of the woods, I told her, "You know... God is weird." She asked me what I meant by that, and I found it a little difficult to explain. According to Christianity, the largest religion in the United States and the one with which the majority of people in this country are most familiar, myself included, God sent his son, Jesus – who is not really his son at all, but the second piece of a three-part composite deity that also includes the

Holy Spirit – to Earth to be horribly tortured and brutally murdered to atone for the sins of mankind.

Now, this bloody sacrifice so vividly portrayed in that controversial movie not only was designed to show us all how much God (Jesus) loves us, but it also was somehow necessary to keep us all from going to hell.

We are, each and every one of us, born to be sinners, the Holy Bible tells us. Not worthy of the love and good graces of the God who created us. And this is all thanks to a couple of people named Adam and Eve, who were successfully tempted by Satan disguised as a serpent to go against God's wishes and commit the most fateful transgression in history by eating an apple from the tree of knowledge in the famous Garden of Eden. Their moment of weakness, act of rebellion or whatever it was, destroyed paradise, condemned all of their descendants forever and ever to lead sin-filled lives, and also inflicted the curse of painful childbirth on women, if I remember my childhood Sunday school training correctly.

And, remember, God knew way ahead of time all of that was going to happen. It was part of his "plan."

But back to Jesus for a moment. Preachers always use the example of a father sending a child to certain death to illustrate the magnitude of God's love for us. He "gave us" his only son. But wait a minute... unlike a human father, God knew for a fact that his son would be back, right? Of course he did, my pastor friend says, but what about the fact that he had to watch his child undergo incredible agony and horrific pain before he died and returned to heaven? Any father that could do that would have to have a tremendous amount of love for those he intends the sacrifice to "save".

Maybe. But what a *strange* plan to begin with. Ordering your son to allow himself to be savagely beaten and nailed through the hands and feet to a cross to die an excruciating death, so that you then could go ahead and forgive the assorted major and minor wrongdoings of all the little human beings you created to worship you, and welcome them joyously back home. Huh? Wrongdoings you knew they were destined to commit when you created them? Bizarre. Nevertheless, for some reason, Jesus dying on the cross supposedly allows us all to have life after death and go back to live forever with God in heaven.

But wait, there's a catch.

To avail yourself of that blessing, you must be a Christian, a follower of Jesus Christ. If you are not, or if you follow any other religious belief – Islam, Judaism, Hinduism, Buddhism – you ain't getting in. You ain't gonna make it. Why? Because you don't follow the Christian belief of Jesus dying on the cross for your salvation. No matter what you do here on Earth, no matter how much love you show others or how many good deeds you perform, your spirit will be doomed and heaven's gate will be locked.

The same God who is brimming with so much love, the one who created you and knew before you were born whether you would or would not follow the right path, will send you to hell when you die and not think twice about it. Adios. If you don't believe the right things during your life, the same Jesus who made the ultimate sacrifice to save us all will turn his head and say, "I never knew you," and toss you into an eternal lake of fire.

I don't know... that just does not make a whole lot of sense.

On the other hand, just because it does not make sense to me, does not mean it is not true. It very well may be true. I don't know. But like I said, I do believe wholeheartedly in some sort of God, and I will tell you why.

Back in 1989, I was a sick man. Physically, emotionally and spiritually sick. I stand a little over 6-1 and weigh around 190 to195 pounds. At that time, I weighed probably 135 to 140 pounds. I could easily wrap my thumb and middle finger around my wrist and slide that circle all the way up to my bicep without the fingertips coming apart. A girl I rented a room from for several months in Houston, after my first wife chased me away, made fun of me from time to time, because her arms were bigger than mine – and she was not a big girl. Hi, Callie.

I suffered blackouts, or memory lapses, on a daily basis for years, and routinely endured tremendous headaches, nausea and vomiting. I woke up sometimes in strange places, like on the ground halfway in and out of my open front door, on someone's lawn, on the bathroom floor next to a toilet. Strange bruises appeared on my body. Strange dents appeared on my automobiles.

What was wrong with me?

I was an alcoholic. A falling-down, throwing-up, blackout drunk. Drinking cheap beer by the case, discount wine by the gallon and holding onto sanity by my fingernails. Tired of living and afraid to die.

Alcoholics and addicts talk about having to "hit bottom" before making the decision to seek help and turn their lives around. I had hit bottom a long time before, suffering innumerable humiliations and painful losses -- including the loss of my dignity -- but I continued to cling to my misery until the bitter end, hoping someone would come along and save me from myself. My secret wish was to collapse out in public somewhere, and be taken to a hospital where I would lovingly be taken care of by wonderful, concerned people. Of course, that never happened and the madness continued.

One day, after I moved in February 1989 from Houston to Temple, a town of about 50,000 people halfway between Austin and Waco along Interstate 35, I decided to call the local state mental health offices to tell someone I needed help. The girl who answered the telephone asked me what was wrong, and I told her, "I'm thinking about killing myself." Which was true, but what I really wanted was for the pain to stop. Her response was not helpful.

"Well… that's not good," she said. No shit, lady, I thought, before hanging up and going back home to get drunk.

I was living then in a tiny, one-bedroom apartment furnished with two sleeping bags on the living room floor and a black-and-white portable television set with a bent coat hanger for an antennae. I had some clothes in the closet, two or three plastic plates, a few plastic cups, forks and spoons, my grandfather's old recliner and my guitar, which I hadn't played in years.

That little apartment was the end of a long road that began back at Scarborough Junior-Senior High School in Houston, Texas, my hometown. It was there that I discovered the joys of chemically altering my consciousness, back in 11th grade.

I was a really intense all-America type kid who made straight 'As' in school without really trying, and played and excelled in sports the whole time I was growing up. First, it was baseball and football at the Oaks Dads Club, where I became an all-star curveball pitcher and a standout running back, quarterback and defensive end. My father coached my teams or helped coach most of the time, and we won several championships in what was a very competitive, talented youth sports program on Houston's near northwest side.

When I got to junior high, I started playing basketball and running track. Our 220-yard relay team went to the regional championships in 7th grade, and I earned a starting spot at guard on the 9th grade basketball team when I was in 8th grade.

But that all came to a screeching halt by the time I was a sophomore, due to a combination of burnout, injury, bad coaching, bad attitude and peer pressure. Basketball was the last sport I quit. After sitting on the bench for what I considered one too many games, I walked into the coach's office and tossed my uniform on his desk. Told him I was quitting. He just looked at me and said nothing. I walked back out and that was it. Athletic career officially over.

More than that, though, along with throwing away a promising future in sports, I also lost something even more important – my identity.

With baseball, basketball, football and track gone, I had absolutely no idea who or what to be. Athletics had been my life from the time I was eight years old. I measured my entire self-worth on achievement in sports. My friends were all jocks, and I still hung out with them for awhile, but it wasn't the same anymore because I was no longer on the teams. I didn't really fit in.

It wasn't long before I found somewhere else to fit in – with the "freaks." The hippies and wanna-be hippies who stood out in front of the school in the mornings and smoked cigarettes and gave the teachers a hard time in class and had loose, good-looking girlfriends and always seemed to be having a good time. All I had to do to be a part of that crowd was grow my hair long and smoke dope. So that's what I did.

The first time I got stoned – watching the Jerry Lewis Labor Day telethon on TV at a friend's house -- I knew I had found the answer. I liked the way it made me feel, and I liked how easy it was to be accepted by all those 'cool' people. I didn't drink much at all in high school, but I was an instant pothead. Smoked pot every day. And by the time I graduated, I was into other drugs as well. And I liked it all.

Along the way, though, my drug of choice eventually became alcohol. Booze was a friend I could always count on and would never let me down, or so I thought. By the time I reached that little apartment in Temple – the middle of nowhere for a big-city boy – I was a 31-year-old drunk on probation for DWI, newly divorced, father of a 9-year-old daughter, one step away from living on the streets. Somehow, I had managed to earn a bachelor's degree in journalism two years before from the University of Houston, after quitting my job as an electrical draftsman for a worldwide engineering company and going back to school full-time. All that time, I considered myself a "functioning alcoholic," because I was still functioning. I often went to work with paralyzing hangovers, and was loaded or hung over for many of my classes at UH, but being a good alcoholic and lifelong perfectionist, I still managed to excel.

By now, though, I was more of a "barely functioning" alcoholic. A co-worker later told me that shortly after I went to work as a reporter for the daily newspaper in Temple, my editor started to figure out that I might have a drinking problem. He was tipped off by someone who called him after I went out to cover a story and arrived at my destination reeking of beer. I never went anywhere in my car – before, during or after work -- without a quart of beer. The only thing that changed after I was arrested for DWI the previous fall was that I started faithfully wearing my seat belt.

Wait, I take that back. One other thing changed, but that was only after I moved to Temple. When I got there, one of the first things I did was report to the Bell County adult probation office. The probation officer took a look at my file and asked if I had been attending Alcoholics Anonymous meetings down in Houston, as I had been ordered to do following an evaluation by the courts there. When I told him no, he told me in no uncertain terms that I would now be attending AA meetings, if I wanted to avoid being sent back to jail. He wrote down an address for the local AA meeting house, and said I could attend the noon 'brown bag' lunch meetings.

I was afraid this old redneck really would send me to jail if I didn't go, so the next day I went looking for the place. It was in a rundown old house on 23rd Street or 25th Street near downtown, with a huge hole in the wooden front porch and a bunch of strange people inside, sitting around a long, narrow table, drinking cups of coffee and smoking cigarettes.

It was indeed a motley crew that attended those meetings – bikers with long hair and cowboy boots, old men with bloodshot eyes and shaky hands, buttoned-up businessmen, grease-covered auto mechanics, middle-aged ladies with manicured nails and luxury cars parked out front, old women with too much lipstick and deep, raspy voices -- but I quickly noticed that most of the stories they told sounded a lot like the stories from my life. I never knew that other people had the same fears, insecurities and other problems that I had. It was truly amazing to me. My whole life, I never talked to anybody about anything. I don't think I ever knew you could do that. In my family growing up, we never talked about *anything*. Certainly not about problems, feelings, emotions.

After about three months of going to my court-ordered quota of eight meetings a month, still drinking heavily every day, I finally threw in the towel and admitted I needed help. I woke up one morning after a particularly brutal three-day binge, hung over and sicker than I had ever been, unable to even drink a sip of water without it coming right back up. It's a little hazy now, but I think I went to an AA meeting that night and introduced myself for the first time as an alcoholic. You know, "Hi, my name is John, and I'm an alcoholic." It was May 22, 1989.

I went home after the meeting, walked into my bedroom, knelt down and started to pray. I said something like, "God, if you're out there somewhere, please help me. I want to stop drinking and stop being so unhappy." Something simple like that. I don't remember all the words exactly, but the thing I do remember is that I was very sincere. Sincerity born of desperation. The words came straight from my heart. I was pleading. I didn't know what else to do.

After I prayed, I walked back into the living room and sat on my $50 thrift-store couch to read a book I had found recently at the public library. Walking up and down the aisles, scanning titles, this book seemed to jump out at me, and it was the story of a former New York Times reporter's recovery from alcoholism through the AA program. Probably just a coincidence that I happened upon that particular book out of the thousands of other volumes in that library. Yeah, just a coincidence.

As I sat there reading, I suddenly was overcome by a feeling of peace and serenity. Time seemed to slow down as I read something about 'selfishness,' and I was wrapped in sort of a warm, fuzzy glow. And I felt something like a hand gently touch the top of my head, and all these twisted knots of pain and confusion, anger and bitterness, seemed to be slowly pulled up and out of my body. This sensation went on for a while, and when the last knot was gone, I felt very relaxed and peaceful, and a little voice inside told me, "Everything's going to be all right." I did not hear an audible voice –

it was more of a feeling. I somehow knew that I did not have to drink anymore.

It is not fashionable in AA circles for a person to say they are "cured" of alcoholism. Every recovering alcoholic, it is said, is one drink away from relapse. True enough, but in my case, instead of having to fight the urge to drink, I am one of the lucky ones whose compulsion was completely removed. Before that extraordinary night when some kind of higher power abruptly ended my drinking problem, I woke up each morning thinking about when I was going to have that first drink. A typical day for me was spent either drinking, thinking about drinking or going to get something to drink. Sometimes I had beer for breakfast. I had absolutely no control over my compulsion to consume alcohol. And one drink always led to another. Always. I got drunk and made a fool of myself the first time I drank alcohol, a scene that was repeated countless times over the ensuing years. My brain just does not have one of those things that says, "That's enough." I could never get enough.

But since that day when the miracle happened, I have never once had the physical craving or mental urge to drink. I've been through plenty of ups and downs during the past 15 years – relationship problems, financial crisis, family feuds, my ex-wife abruptly moving our 15-year-old daughter across the country, and my mother's slow death from brain cancer – but through all those things, I never was tempted to drink alcohol or use drugs.

I remember standing in my kitchen one morning shortly after I sobered up, leaning against the counter, drinking a cup of coffee, when it dawned on me that I was not hung over, and I remembered everything I had done the night before. "Hey," I told myself, "I didn't drink last night, did I?" It was truly a strange feeling. A month or two after that, I was on my way back from the local convenience store one evening, walking through the apartment complex, when I happened to look up at the clear, star-filled sky and marveled at the fact that not only was I sober and clear-headed, I was carrying a 12-pack of soft drinks.

So that is why I believe in God. I can never deny what happened to me that night. I was suddenly and permanently cured of a terrible addiction, a misery from which many people never recover. There was no one else in that room, except some kind of force that reached deep inside me and healed at least part of my soul. I don't know what else it could have been, except for God.

Some might suggest that what happened was not God at all. Scientists tell us that we humans generally use only a small percentage (10 percent?) of our brain capacity, and so maybe the intensity of my prayer and concentration somehow tapped into a portion of my unused brainpower, my "higher self," and that is the real source of my miracle. Could be. But maybe it is the power of God that dwells inside that higher self. Maybe that higher self is where God lives, and maybe our job here on Earth is to learn how to tap into that source of positive energy and healing he provides, and perform our own miracles. Maybe that is what the Bible means when it says that someone who has the faith of a mustard seed can literally move mountains.

After all, it is hard, if not impossible, to look around at the world and imagine that it was not created by some kind of higher power. Why was it created? I don't know. But the incredible beauty and variety that exists all around us in nature... all of that just evolved haphazardly?

And what about the human body? Such a complex, sturdy and yet fragile piece of machinery just developed on its own? From – what was it, pond scum? Take something as small as the human ear, for example. All those tiny bones and things, fitting intricately and perfectly together in such a way that invisible waves of energy riding through the air are amplified and recognized in the brain as laughter, speech, thunder... and music.

Ah, music. Ask a songwriter or composer how they go about writing songs – where do those words and melodies come from? Many will say the music comes from God, and is floating freely around the universe. Occasionally, a piece of it collides with a musician and, voila! A song is born.

After spending about three years as an active member of a small, evangelical Christian church, I gradually became more and more disillusioned with what I saw as extreme narrow-mindedness and intolerance toward other belief systems. Some call it religious bigotry. The God who saved the life of a wretch like me is not the same one who allows people to suffer immense pain and horrible deaths because "it is his will," part of the plan. Or the same one who condemns billions of souls to eternal damnation because they take the wrong road to try to find him.

I don't know what God is. I would like to believe in the vision of some sort of handsome, heavenly king, seated on a magnificent bejeweled throne, surrounded by singing angels who welcome me to a golden paradise when I die. A glorious reunion with my creator, and all my family members and friends who preceded me in death. An eternal celebration with no more pain or sorrow. I know that belief is what sustains and comforts millions of people around the world, but I just cannot honestly accept that idea in my heart of hearts. Why not? Lots of reasons, I guess. Too many inconsistencies in the story. Too many questions, with too few answers that make any sense. Why are one person's prayers answered, and another's are not? Why do people suffer such agony during their lives? So that they will turn to God for comfort and give their lives to him, the way he wants them to? How cruel that seems.

But I do see the hand of some divine, creative force all around me, all the time. I see it when a sunrise streaks the sky with red, orange and yellow, as I stand with friends in the cool waters of the Gulf of Mexico. I see it as I stand in my driveway, trying to find various planets and twinkling stars in the vast, awe-inspiring nighttime sky. It is there when I find a new flower in my yard, blooming some impossibly rich, achingly beautiful color in a spot where I don't remember ever planting anything. I hear God in the tender voice of singing children. I see God in the face of another human being who shows me love when I do not deserve to be loved.

During my travels around the state looking for people to interview for this book, I encountered a number of what a friend refers to as "God things." In El Paso, a city I had never visited before and knew nothing about, I happened to drive by a church on a Tuesday morning and see a number of cars in the parking lot. So I pulled in, parked and walked into the office. A frail-looking man wearing denim shorts and a wrinkled T-shirt, his arms and legs covered with tattoos and scars, was there. I knew instinctively that I was looking at someone with a story to tell. However, he politely declined my request for an interview and sent me upstairs.

I thanked him and left. After finding no one on the second floor willing to sit down with me and talk about spirituality, I was on my way back out the door when the guy from the office downstairs stopped me and said he changed his mind and would be glad to talk. That guy was Chris Hensley, a remarkable example of God's love.

Sister Margie, a Catholic nun in Marfa, blew me away with her views on heaven and hell, and her belief that there are different truths, and more than one way to get to heaven. That and her glowing spirit that absolutely radiated warmth and love.

So, I continue my spiritual journey, my search for meaning, trying to find answers that make sense. And traveling hundreds of miles back and forth across Texas, asking all different kinds of people what they think about God, was an enlightening, humbling part of that journey that enriched my life forever. It was an honor and a privilege to meet them, to share a few moments of their lives and then to tell their stories.

About a month before I started this project in the summer of 2004, I finished reading the autobiography of Boy George, a highly flamboyant, cross-dressing pop singer from the 1980s, and in that book I discovered an excellent perspective on the search for meaning. After recovering from a horrendous drug addiction, George underwent his own spiritual transformation. And according to the one-time atheist, "The search for God is the search for yourself."

Julie Palmer of Houston told me pretty much the same thing – that when we are able to look deep within ourselves and accept our own truths, good and bad, we will find God there waiting for us. Chris Sammons of Nacogdoches said that if we search long and hard enough, eventually God will reveal himself to us in a way that makes sense.

I believe I found God once, that night 15 years ago when I cried out in desperation for help. For some reason, he decided to grant me a miracle. And something was certainly watching over me all those years I was drinking and drugging myself into oblivion. I also have witnessed the births of both of my daughters, even cutting the umbilical cord attached to my youngest. Some say newborn babies are the closest to God we can get here on Earth. I sat on the front porch of a tiny barbershop on the outskirts of Lufkin, looking into the eyes of a World War II veteran as he told me about an angel who saved his life during the Battle of the Bulge. A pharmacist-turned-pastor from Longview took my hands in his and prayed for my success after relating the story of a life-changing conversation, in which he says he literally heard the voice of God speaking to him as he prayed and meditated in his living room. Another man looked me in the eye as we sat in his tree-shaded, downtown area home during a brewing midday thunderstorm and said with the utmost sincerity and gravity that, in a past life, he was Jesus Christ.

As I said, all the stories and testimonies I heard during my travels were fascinating, often touching and sometimes heart-wrenching. I heard a lot of things I agreed with, and a lot of things with which I do not agree. One of the things I found most reassuring, though, was when I asked someone a tough question about heaven and hell, life and death, and the answer they gave me was, "I don't know." Not some automatic cookie-cutter response, quotation from scripture, or textbook interpretation. Just a simple, "I don't know."

Because in the end, nobody really knows. Some of my die-hard Christian friends tell me that what is most important in the search for truth is what is in one's heart. And in my heart, I think there is more than one right path in this journey to wherever it is we are all going. I hope so. I just don't see a loving, beautifully creative God condemning so many souls to a torturous eternity. Why would he do such a thing?

The only firm conclusion I have reached thus far is this: I ain't worried about it. Like my close friend, Jim McBrayer, I have stopped worrying about whether I am going to heaven or hell when I die. Of course, that may all change as I get older, but right now, I really don't believe in a place called hell, because I really don't believe that a loving God would send me or anyone else there, simply because I consider the notion that Christianity does not have a monopoly on the truth. As far as heaven, who knows? What is heaven, anyway? And, besides, I don't play the harp and I'm not a very good singer. I sure hope they have golf in heaven. And I would like to meet John Lennon, and see Jimi Hendrix play the guitar, with Keith Moon on drums, John Entwhistle on bass, and Janis Joplin and Jim Morrison on vocals.

My wife tells me I am too irreverent when it comes to God. I think he not only knows my heart, but God also has a sense of humor. And Pastor Sammons told me that it is OK to ask the tough questions. I certainly hope so. God did, after all, create me the way I am, right?

About the Author

John Henry Clark III is an award-winning journalist, freelance writer, author and avid golfer who was born and raised in Texas. He grew up in northwest Houston playing sports at Oaks Dads Club and attending church with his parents, but decided as he got older that things he learned in Sunday school no longer made much sense.

Since then, he has spent a lifetime seeking answers and exploring a variety of beliefs. After a successful career as a newspaper reporter, Clark turned his lifetime love for learning into a new career as a public school teacher, and that gave him time during the summer months to pursue his project to research and write a book describing what people believe about God and why they believe what they believe.

That effort turned into the book, *Finding God: An Exploration of Spiritual Diversity in America's Heartland*. A tireless seeker, researcher and questioner, John has written a number of other fascinating books dealing with the human experience, from tragedies to triumphs and more, including *Camino: Laughter and Tears along Spain's 500-mile Camino de Santiago*. To read more of John's books, find answers to the meaning of life, and maybe discover something new about yourself, go here: http://amzn.to/1EmgWa7

Made in the USA
San Bernardino, CA
07 January 2018